D1237840

55

30¢

SAVING IN A FREE SOCIETY

A

INSTITUTE OF ECONOMIC AFFAIRS

The Institute was formed in 1957 as a research and educational trust that specialises in the study of markets and pricing systems as technical devices for registering preferences and apportioning resources. Micro-economic analysis forms the kernel of economics and is relevant and illuminating independently of the social or political framework: in the public and private sectors, and in collectivist and individualist societies. Where the macro-economic method is used its results are verified and interpreted in the light of micro-economic analysis.

The Institute's work is assisted by an advisory council which includes:

Colin Clark
Professor Stanley Dennison
Dr R. F. Henderson
Graham Hutton
Professor John Jewkes
Professor E. Victor Morgan

Professor Alan T. Peacock
G. J. Ponsonby
Professor A. R. Prest
George Schwartz
Henry Smith
Professor Jack Wiseman

Professor B. S. Yamey

General Director
Ralph Harris

Editorial Director
Arthur Seldon

Secretary and Treasurer
G. E. Blundell

Research
Hamish Gray

Publications Manager
Michael Solly

The Institute is independent of any political party or group. It is financed partly by sales of its publications and partly by voluntary contributions. Subscription is open to all interested individuals and organisations; full details are obtainable from the Secretary.

THE INSTITUTE OF ECONOMIC AFFAIRS LTD.
EATON HOUSE, 66A EATON SQUARE, LONDON, SW1
Telephone BELGRAVIA 2294

Saving in a
Free Society

J. ENOCH POWELL

M.B.E., M.P.

Southern Baptist College
FELIX GOODSON
LIBRARY
Walnut Ridge, Ark.

Published by

THE INSTITUTE OF ECONOMIC AFFAIRS

1966

THE INSTITUTE OF ECONOMIC AFFAIRS
66A EATON SQUARE, LONDON, SW1

First published 1960
Second Edition 1966

© The Institute of Economic Affairs 1960, 1966

All rights reserved

Printed in Great Britain by
ROWAN PRESS LTD., LEAVESDEN, WATFORD, HERTS.

22,545

339.4
871s

Contents

TABLES AND CHARTS

TABLES

CHARTS

INTRODUCTION

The larger part of this book consists of a description of the experience of saving generally, and of various channels of saving in particular, during the last fifteen or so years in Britain. It would scarcely have been useful to attempt to carry the description farther back: the decade of the Second World War and its aftermath is not comparable with the 1950s or 1960s; and before 1939 most of the measurements and statistics relevant to saving are either not available or very imperfect.

To compare the United Kingdom's experience in detail with that of other Western countries would be a rewarding undertaking, but only if the data from each country studied and the comparisons between them were informed by a thorough knowledge of local circumstances and local differences. Otherwise the exercise would be more misleading than informative. To do justice to it, the co-operation of a whole team of workers would be necessary.

Indeed, even within the narrower limits of this study, I would be the last to suppose that I have done more than describe the salient features and draw attention to aspects which seem to be significant and deserving of closer investigation. The dearth of detailed academic and statistical study of saving is surprising and ought to be remedied. I hope this essay may help to attract attention to a somewhat neglected field.

Before attempting to describe the actual behaviour of saving, on however limited a scale, it was necessary to seek some clarity on what saving is. Here the difficulty is not the dearth of theoretical discussion but its abundance. The notion of saving lies near the heart of the greatest economic controversies of the last thirty years, if not longer, and the layman is conscious of treading a field which, if not prohibited to angels, has been fought over by giants.

But though daunted, he has no choice but to enter if he wishes to provide himself with the apparatus for forming an opinion on matters of current economic debate. The decisions of policy, for example, which are embodied in the annual Budget turn to no small extent upon the concept of saving—not only how much saving may be expected in given circumstances, but what saving itself means and what its economic implications are. Hence at the moment of plunging into this Minotaur's labyrinth, I have attempted to make

7

fast at the entrance the Ariadne thread of definition. In doing so, I am aware that I have grossly over-simplified, ignoring all manner of modifications and subtleties.

Economics merge into politics as soon as the endeavour to describe what does happen or has happened is tinged with a view of what ought to have happened or ought to happen henceforward. While I have done my best to be objective in definition and description, my approach to decision is frankly partisan. I happen to believe that when a society's economic life ceases to be shaped by the interaction of the free decisions of individuals, freedom is in a fair way to disappear from other sides of its existence as well. The terms 'free economy' and 'free society' are to me interchangeable. That being so, I believe that a society's behaviour in saving as in the rest of its economic activity is best determined by the mechanisms of free decision; and I have not avoided stating some of the reasons for this belief and some of the conclusions for policy to which it leads me.

In the first edition of this book I acknowledged the enjoyment and profit I had drawn from the advice and instruction of the late Sir Dennis Robertson. He had no responsibility for anything in this book, but it owed him a great debt.

J. ENOCH POWELL

House of Commons
May 1966

★   ★   ★

We wish to thank Mrs Barbara Marlow for her work in revising the Tables and redrawing the Charts, which she devised originally for the first edition of this book.

IEA

Part I

An Anatomy of Saving

'The economist does not make new difficulties. He merely brings into prominence some that are latent in everyday discourse. The trouble of examining them in a good light is worth what it costs; for it saves constant confusion of thought.'

Alfred Marshall, *Elements of Economics*, Vol. I, p. 49.

CHAPTER I

THE MEANING OF SAVING

Much political and popular discussion of saving is vitiated by faulty definition. The word has several distinct meanings in common use; and it is not uncommon to find one substituted for another in the course of the same argument or even the same sentence.[1] It is therefore indispensable to begin by definition and distinction.

'Saving' is a verbal noun. Its meaning and economic effect depend in part on who is the subject of the implied verb 'to save'.

1. The Individual

It is simplest to begin with the case where the subject is an individual who disposes of an income. Such an individual may be said to dispose of his income in one of two ways: he may 'consume' it, or he may 'save' it. The distinction between the two is fundamentally one of *time*. If I receive sixpence as income and instantly spend it on an iced lolly which I instantly swallow, that is no doubt consumption. If I keep the sixpence in my pocket, even though a day—or a month, or a year—and later I still use it to buy and eat a lolly, have I not meantime saved it?

---

[1]Take for instance the following passage in a reputable periodical:
"The Budget gave a potential £366 million of additional purchasing power for the current financial year. Not all this will be spent. Extra *savings* by companies and individuals could amount to as much as £100 million, and in any case will need to be substantial if the Government is to cover its overall deficit of £720 million at all comfortably. However, we can estimate that the actual purchasing power released by the Budget is £250 million."
In order to make sense of this passage, 'savings' must be understood first as 'income retained in the form of cash', then as 'income lent to the Government' and finally again as 'income retained in the form of cash'. Neither meaning is the general, accepted or natural one.

11

FELIX GOODSON LIBRARY

Again, suppose I buy with current income three one-shilling tins of baked beans, consume one with all possible haste and leave the other two in the larder for a year before using them. Surely I have saved the two tins just as much as I should have saved the two shillings if I kept them by me in cash? Indeed, in any economy which dispenses with the use of money—in a primitive barter system, or even in the animal world—saving must take place by way of accumulating articles for later consumption.

Thus the first point which we notice about consumption and saving is that the distinction between them can be made only in relation to *a specific period* of time: it is a distinction between two methods of laying out within a period of time the income received within that same[1] period of time.

In the examples of disposal by consumption considered so far, the nature of the consumption was crudely physical and rapid. But this is not necessary. The essential idea is the laying out of income to obtain satisfaction from it in the relevant period—excepting only one kind of satisfaction, that which arises from the act of saving itself, i.e. from denying oneself all other satisfactions. When a tycoon purchases out of income a picture to adorn his gallery, there is 'consumption' on his part as there is 'consumption' on the part of a labourer who buys a loaf of bread with part of his wages: it is not necessary that the means of satisfaction should themselves be 'consumed' in the sense of being used up.

Nevertheless, the difference between a source of satisfaction of short duration (such as a loaf of bread) and one of long duration (such as an old master) is important. Since the distinction between saving and consumption refers to a period of time, the acquisition from income of a source of satisfaction which will continue to produce that satisfaction after the end of the relevant period must, to that extent, be saving. A clear example is the purchase of houseroom. If out of a year's income I buy a 10-year lease, then approximately nine years' worth of the price is 'saved': only the part attributable to the shelter and privacy enjoyed in the current year, equivalent to a current payment of rent, is 'consumed'. In some kinds of outlay the ratio of current to future satisfaction is so low that for practical

---

[1] Or rather, because outlay can never coincide absolutely with receipt, an equal but slightly anterior period. The qualification, however, is of little practical importance unless the period is a very short one.

purposes the entire outlay may be regarded as saving. This applies, for instance, to the freehold of substantial buildings and especially of land.

Many kinds of asset are such that outlay of income in acquiring them is unambiguous: purchase of an iced lolly is objectively recognisable as consumption, and purchase of a savings certificate as saving. With many other assets, however, the distinction between consumption and saving is *subjective*: it depends on the intention with which the outlay is made and not on the nature of the object acquired. Let us again take the example of a house. Of two persons buying a house out of income, one may do so with the purpose of current enjoyment (consumption) as well as of future enjoyment (saving). The other may do so with the purpose of selling it in the future at the same or an enhanced price, or of deriving from it a rent which he can enjoy as income. The latter, if he occupies no part of the house, is engaged entirely in saving.

Of course the intention may be changed before it is carried, or carried fully, into effect: a purchase may be made with the object of consumption and then for some reason or another the consumption may not take place. If so, the outlay has passed from the category of consumption to that of saving, or conversely.

The individual, then, saves that part of his income which he does not lay out with the intention of procuring a satisfaction during the period of time chosen for relating the receipt and the outlay of the income.

His saving may be classified according to his motive, if any, in refraining from consumption. One motive may be simply to defer consumption. If so, the intention is to 'dis-save' in a later period what is saved in the present period. It may be desired to defer consumption to a 'rainy day' of sickness or old age or to a time (or place) where tins of beans are harder to come by.

Where the saving does not take place in the form of the actual consumption goods themselves, there may be the subsidiary motive of increasing consumption as well as deferring it; and, of course, this result can also occur unsought. It can happen where the conversion value of the savings rises, or where they are in a form on which interest accrues. For example, people join a Christmas club in order to increase, as well as to defer, consumption; and when they accumulate savings in the form of savings certificates with a specific expenditure or contingency in view, the prospective increase in the value of the savings may nevertheless be present to their mind as a subsidiary motive.

On the other hand, no dis-saving may be contemplated. The motive may be to secure a future income, the saver being concerned with the satisfaction to be obtained from the interest, rent or other 'growing produce' of the savings. Often this motive and the former one are intentionally or unintentionally combined. It has not been uncommon, for instance, for a man to acquire a row of houses by saving out of income and then to live on the rents without making provision for the distant but inevitable hour when they will be untenanted. However, rational and prudent persons will not usually, if they are aware of what they are doing, attempt both to consume the savings and to enjoy the growing produce of them, while they last, as income, unless the risk of surviving the exhaustion of the savings can be spread and thus neutralised, e.g. by the purchase of an annuity from an insurance company.

A third motive can be that of mere accumulation, without any distinct contemplation either of future dis-saving or of future income. A person so wealthy as to be provided (humanly speaking) against all possible contingencies and in receipt of so large an income that further increases (especially after tax) bring little or no satisfaction, may save nevertheless because he enjoys accumulating wealth.

Finally, saving may be passive and unmotivated, arising simply from failure to lay out the whole income of a period on current satisfaction within that period. On some scale, this unintended saving is widespread and, indeed, in the last analysis, virtually unavoidable, though on a large scale it is perhaps the more likely the bigger the income.

2. *A corporation*

A company or other corporate body which receives an income can, like an individual, 'consume' or 'save' it; but the terms have not the same meanings. A corporation is not itself capable of satisfaction. The satisfaction is that of individual human members. The choice confronting a corporation is whether or not to distribute to its members the income becoming available for distribution.[1]

[1] A complication arises where the members of a corporation are themselves corporate bodies; but the ultimate satisfaction is still that of the human individuals who are the members of the latter.

For a corporation the decision to distribute or not (i.e. not to 'save', or to 'save') is always a *deliberate* one. Unlike the individual, who may omit to consume part of his income without any deliberate intention of saving, a corporate body can distribute the whole of its income as easily as a fraction, and cannot avoid deciding the question consciously.

A corporation may admittedly be frightened or cajoled into saving by governmental or public opinion, or persuaded or even forced to save by fiscal or other law. Subject, however, to this qualification, the decision to save or not is made freely and deliberately by the corporate body on behalf of all its members.

A world of meaning lies behind the words 'on behalf of', but a world which fortunately need not be explored or mapped for our present purpose.[1] Suffice it to say, that the decisions of the corporate body are not in any way the sum of those of its members. For instance, they are not necessarily those which would have been reached by a democratic process of voting, whether by heads, by a card vote or by any other principle.[2] Still less are they the decisions to consume or to save which the members would themselves have taken if the whole of the corporation's income had been distributed to them.

A typical statement by a company chairman puts the position very well:[3]

"It has always been our practice in this company to pursue a conservative dividend policy. I have no doubt that it was the right policy, particularly during a period of comparatively rapid expansion such as has taken place since the second World War. But it has meant that the holders of the ordinary shares have in effect been adding to their investment in the company: the undistributed profit *which belongs to them*[4] has become additional capital, and the assets which it represents have been used in the business. This additional capital is just as much entitled

[1] See A. Rubner, *The Ensnared Shareholder*, Macmillan, 1965.
[2] In fact, the articles of association of most companies contain the provision (clause 114) in the model articles attached to the Companies Act, 1948, "that dividend shall be declared in general meeting and that no dividend shall exceed the amount recommended by the Directors". Thus the shareholders can decide by a vote to save more; but they can decide to save less only by changing the Board.
[3] Rugby Portland Cement Company, Annual General Meeting, 1959.
[4] My italics.

to its reward as that more formally designated as issued share capital."

The object which a corporation has in view in deciding between distribution and non-distribution must, in theory at least, be to maximise the income ultimately distributed, taking present and future together; for it is only through distribution that any satisfaction is ever obtained from the corporation's income. But how long a future? and what kind of distribution?

A corporation can, and often does, take a longer view than its members individually, and can thus pursue a policy which aims at increasing the distribution to a future generation of members at the price of reducing that to the present generation.[1] Indeed, very large and powerful corporations (or rather, their human agents and servants) can acquire a kind of personality and *esprit de corps* of their own, with the result that the purpose of benefiting the actual members, present or future, is lost sight of in the purpose of increasing the greatness and importance of the corporation itself. This is the extreme towards which a corporation tends with size and time.

The ultimate distribution of income which the policy of a corporation aims at maximising over a period may take more forms than one. For example, where the income received by members of a corporation as dividend is subject to tax at a higher rate, while that which they receive by realising an enhancement in the value of their share in the corporation's assets is taxed at a lower rate, the object of maximising distribution over a period of time may be achieved partly by maximising the value of those assets. Corporate saving may aim at increased benefit to members *via* capital gains as well as *via* higher dividends.

3. *The state: as government*

The term 'saving' is again completely different in meaning when applied to the state, either in the sense of the government or of the community as a whole.

---

[1] See, for example, the Report of the Chairman of the United Kingdom Provident Institution, 1 March, 1960: "The fact is that life assurance is a continuous business in which each generation benefits by the restraint of its predecessors and in turn should pass on a similar advantage to the next. As the directors see the position, their first duty is to preserve and improve the strength of the funds on which earning power depends".

The income of the government may be regarded as that part of its subjects' gross incomes which it can persuade them to make over to it. By reducing its income and expenditure in the present, it may obtain the means of increasing both in the future; for example, a regime maintaining a large army by means of heavy taxes might, by disbanding it and reducing taxation, enable itself later on to mobilize a still larger army backed by a stronger economy. Thus taxable capacity, and consequently the potential income of the government in the future, may be maximised by avoiding expenditure in the present; and this could be regarded as a form of saving by the state as government.

In a modern state the government's income is virtually all laid out in the year in which it is received: governments do not normally raise taxes in order to store up in some form, such as gold, a surplus of purchasing power, and so carry forward from one year to another the claims on goods and services which their subjects make over to them. In fact a government tries to equate its income with its intended outlay. Part of that outlay may be redistribution, including the repayment of debt. Another part will be the purchase of services and of goods consumed during the period. Yet another part of the outlay, however, may be on assets which remain in its ownership and continue to be useful to it after the end of the period. The part of the revenue thus laid out may fairly be described as having been 'saved' to the extent of the residual value of the assets. In this sense a sum raised in taxation and spent for instance on building government offices, or buying more than a year's normal supply of ink for use in them, represents government saving.

The position of any public authority invested with power to raise a revenue is similar to that of the government itself, except that these subordinate authorities, such as local government bodies, can and sometimes do save considerable fractions of their income at one time or another in the form of cash or realisable assets.

4. *The state: as community*

For a community as a whole, income cannot be other than the total production of goods and services by its members, including what it obtains by exchanging part of its production for that of other communities, and also including the return from assets owned by it or its members which are situated in other communities. This income is described as 'gross' before, and 'net' after, deducting the value of capital consumed in producing it.

Part of a community's production may be exchanged not directly for goods or services from other communities but either for a claim on the future production of those other countries (as with a loan or investment) or else for tokens of value (gold or currencies) which may be exchanged for goods and services in the future. In its external aspect, viewed as a unit in a world populated by other such units, the community can thus save by increasing its reserves of gold and foreign currencies or the indebtedness of other communities to it. Conversely, it dis-saves when it runs those reserves down or diminishes that indebtedness.

Saving by the community in this sense, though important in some of its economic effects, usually represents quantitatively a small fraction of the national income. In the bumper year 1958 the saving of the United Kingdom, in terms of export of goods and services not balanced by imports in the same period, was only a little over 2 per cent of the gross national income.

As applied to the community in its internal aspect, the notions of 'consumption' and 'saving' denote not, as with the individual, different ways of disposing of income, but—because income and production are identical—a classification of income (or production) itself. The distinction is between two categories of production: that which is to supply current satisfaction (i.e. production for consumption), and that which is directly or indirectly to supply future satisfaction. It will be noted that as a community's income includes what is obtained by exchange with other communities but not what is given in exchange, the distinction is also between import for current and import for future satisfaction. Thus, for example, the growing of lettuces which are exchanged for machine tools is production to supply future, not current satisfaction.

In either category more may be produced than is actually applied during the period to supply current satisfaction, or to provide for future satisfaction, respectively. The excess is represented by an increase of stocks, from tins on the housewife's larder shelf to steel bars at the stockists; and this in both cases is a form of saving. In other periods more than the total relevant income may be applied to current satisfaction or to provision for future satisfaction, in which case dis-saving or de-stocking results. Changes in stocks may be the result of deliberate public policy, such as the accumulation of strategic reserves of food or materials, or they may be due to variations in the behaviour of businesses or individuals produced by altered expectations of prices or demand.

Again, variations in stocks, though they can have important economic effects, are usually small in relation to the national income. In the United Kingdom the increases in stocks (including 'work in progress' but excluding stocks with the domestic consumer) were estimated[1] in the last 15 years at the following percentages of the gross national product:

1950	—1.8[2]	1955	1.8	1960	2.6
1951	4.4	1956	1.4	1961	1.3
1952	0.4	1957	1.2	1962	0.3
1953	0.8	1958	0.5	1963	0.7
1954	0.4	1959	0.8	1964	1.9

Foreign trade and stocks are not however the only complications in distinguishing between production which corresponds to consumption and that which corresponds to saving. We also run into the problem of 'durable' goods which cannot be produced without catering for both current and future satisfaction at the same time—the house, the private car, the painting. We encounter many kinds of services which defy classification. What, for instance, of that substantial portion of the national income or production which is represented by education services? It is hard to say that it is in any true sense catering for current consumption, or to deny that it really represents investment for future consumption and future production. Yet no one classifies this expenditure as saving.

In practice we restrict (but should be conscious that we do so artificially) our definition of the community's saving to the increase of stocks and 'fixed capital'; and in the latter we arbitrarily include one type of durable consumption goods, and one only—housing—and ignore the element in all other consumption goods (cars, furniture, etc.) which provides for satisfaction beyond the current period. Even with these restrictions, the definition is imperfect until we have deducted from the total of fixed capital produced, that part of it which goes to replace the fixed capital used up during the period, that is,

[1]*National Income and Expenditure* 1965, Tables 1 and 6.
[2]I.e., stocks were reduced.

until the distinction has been made between the community's gross and net production of fixed capital.

The distinction is easy to state in principle, but impossible to carry through precisely in practice. What proportion, for instance, of the houses built this year are merely replacing others which are demolished or have fallen out of occupation? The answer depends not only on the numbers pulled down or abandoned, but on assumptions about the average rate of obsolescence of existing houses, not to mention a subjective judgment upon the quality and value of the new as compared with the old. Again, who can say what part of the cost of new factories and plants for producing artificial fabrics and plastics represents the replacement of existing cotton mills that are closed or abandoned? Continuous change in the pattern of production makes it impossible to define the extent to which the instruments of production in one period should be regarded as replacements of those employed

TABLE I

INCREASE IN FIXED CAPITAL AND STOCKS:
1948 to 1964

£ million

Year	Gross national product	Gross fixed capital formation and increase in stocks	Capital consumption	Column 2 minus column 3	Column 4 as %age of column 1
	1	2	3	4	5
1948	10,526	1,597	848	749	7·1
1949	11,142	1,642	893	749	6·7
1950	11,745	1,490	953	537	4·6
1951	12.974	2,464	1,101	1,363	10·5
1952	14,030	2,156	1,240	916	6·5
1953	15,080	2,484	1,289	1,195	7·9
1954	15,937	2,608	1,340	1,268	8·0
1955	16,945	3,097	1,461	1,636	9·7
1956	18,421	3,354	1,584	1,770	9·6
1957	19,516	3,608	1,691	1,917	9·8
1958	20,375	3,578	1,791	1,787	8·8
1959	21,376	3,887	1,844	2,043	9·6
1960	22,768	4,696	1,933	2,763	12·1
1961	24,335	4,895	2,065	2,830	11·6
1962	25,409	4,739	2,198	2,541	10·0
1963	27,003	5,094	2,323	2,771	10·3
1964	28,910	6,328	2,458	3,870	13·4

Source: *National Income and Expenditure*, 1965.

in an earlier period. Needless to say, depreciation charges in money terms for tax purposes are less than adequate as a guide, particularly during periods of inflation, when the cost of replacing identical equipment may rise sharply.

Table I shows the net increase in fixed capital and stocks each year since 1948 in the United Kingdom as a percentage of gross national product, using the same figures for capital consumption as are used by the Central Statistical Office in their estimates. Only subject to the very large qualifications discussed above can this increase be regarded as in any sense representing the part of the national income which the community has saved.

CHAPTER II

HOW MUCH SAVING?

If we ask the question: 'Is saving a good thing, and if so, how much of it?' we find once again, as with saving itself, that the question has a different meaning and a different answer according to whether it is considered from the point of view of an individual, a corporation or a community.

1. *Personal saving*

To ask whether saving by the individual, or personal saving, is a good thing from his point of view, might seem a superfluous question, to be answered with a simple and unqualified affirmative. The moral as well as practical benefits of saving to the individual are, and always have been, almost an article of religious conviction among whole classes of citizens. To read the history of the movements and institutions which encourage and facilitate individual saving is to see how the virtues and advantages of thrift have been assumed without question or qualification.

In reality the subject is complex, difficult and full of paradox. Assuming self-control to be a virtue, and assuming that self-control is employed when a man refrains from consuming his income within a given period, then saving is the practice of a virtue. But this is to take saving outside the economic sphere and value it by other standards. Economic benefit lies in consumption; and saving is a good thing (economically) for the individual precisely in so far and only in so far as it gives him the most desirable level of consumption over the span of his existence.

The man who has saved 'for a rainy day' continues to consume at or near his usual standard while the metaphorical rain lasts. The man who has saved for retirement continues to consume at or near his usual standard when he no longer earns a current income. The man who saves at interest and in such a way that his savings increase in value can achieve a greater total consumption than if he had not saved.

These advantages, however, are fully secured by the individual only if his saving is matched by eventual dis-saving. This fact is recognised in common parlance: he who saves without the object of consuming the fruits of his saving is not praised for his thrift but condemned as a miser. Of course, since the span of an individual's existence is uncertain, and the incidence of 'rainy days' unpredictable, the individual's dis-saving will equal his saving only by accident. In practice, when people save against contingencies, the danger of being found to have under-estimated future needs frequently outweighs in their minds the disadvantage of an extra sacrifice of present consumption and so produces a tendency for the individual saver to over-provide.

This tendency is, however, offset by the institution of insurance, which, by pooling risks, enables the individual saver to limit the amount of his saving to something near the dis-saving actually required—not in his own individual case but as an average over the whole field of those insured. *A fortiori* the individual's advantage from saving against contingencies is reduced or even extinguished by community provision for them. For example, the establishment of the National Health Service has greatly reduced the advantage of individual saving—either directly or by way of insurance—against the contingency of having to pay doctors' and hospital bills. The same is true, to varying degrees, of all the social services, from subsidised university education to national assistance.

Leaving aside, however, the qualifications introduced by insurance and over-insurance, the fact remains that, from the individual's point of view as an individual, income saved which is not sooner or later balanced by dis-saving is income wasted. No doubt in real life comparatively few individuals take a purely *individual* point of view. The earner in a family normally seeks to lay out his income to the best economic advantage of the family as a unit, and of all its members as individuals. He may, for example, rationally refrain from present consumption so that half a century after his ashes have been laid to rest, the youngest of his daughters can still be living in spinster comfort on an annuity. In such a case, the span of existence and the contingencies against which the saver provides are those of the family, so far as he identifies its advantage with his own or even substitutes it for himself.

This extension of the individual saver's personality may go so far and wide that the implicit dis-saving is pushed into a remote and vague futurity. The merchant who saves to 'found a family' is first imagining, and then identifying himself with, his distant descendants for centuries to come, and hopes when dying amid his amassed savings to exclaim with Goethe's Faust: 'In the presentiment of happiness so great, I now enjoy my finest hour'. At some point on the gamut which runs from the purely individual view to this sublimated vision, economic motive has been overlaid and replaced by non-economic motives and we approach that sphere of altruism in which men sacrifice their all for their fatherland or their god. The transition is a gradual one: we cannot say with precision at what point saving has ceased to be an economic advantage to the individual saver.

These are not the only reasons why people indulge in excess saving from the individual's point of view, i.e. in saving not matched by dis-saving. Many of the most desirable forms of consumption are catered for by the possession of goods so durable that they are virtually certain to survive those who acquire them. In such cases the consumer has no choice but to do a considerable amount of excess saving in order to secure the consumption which he wishes. Inevitably a great part of this saving 'runs to waste' from his point of view. If I want to live in a fine house with pictures and a sumptuous library, even though I have no issue and no care for posterity, I should need to take elaborate precautions if I wanted to avoid a great deal of wasted saving. I must, for example, sell these possessions subject to a life interest and endeavour to consume the proceeds of the sale as income.

Yet even here I am thwarted—and thwarted by a powerful force, that of vanity. Consumption in forms which imply affluence is robbed of part of its satisfaction unless accompanied by the consciousness of exclusive possession of the source of it, and, what is still more important, the consciousness that the world is aware of that exclusive possession. The satisfaction of using a car, inhabiting a house, contemplating an old master, is lessened if the right to do so is paid for by instalments or otherwise secured by any title short of ownership. The kind of consumption, in fact, which is inseparable from possession of highly durable goods will normally involve saving not matched by dis-saving.

Beyond this point lies the sheer instinct of accumulation and acquisition. This instinct is strong and ought not to be under-estimated in accounting for people's behaviour in regard to consumption and saving. It may well be at least as important as any distinct aim or rational motive, and in obeying it men can be said to be satisfying a requirement of their nature.

Finally, there is the involuntary saving which occurs where a person's income exceeds what he cares to spend upon consumption. In such a case it would be a greater sacrifice to consume more, than it is to refrain from consumption: the effort devoted to discovering and satisfying additional needs for consumption would actually represent an economic loss. If my highest idea of bliss is to live in college and read, write and even acquire books on patristic theology, then, unless my income is very small indeed, I am unlikely to maximise my satisfaction without saving, i.e. without avoiding the nuisance of consuming, some part of it. The case is not as uncommon as might be supposed.

Yet, however widely the notion of the individual is drawn, and however variously his advantage is interpreted, there is still something profoundly artificial in attempting to decide purely from the standpoint of the individual whether saving is a good thing, and how much of it. The welfare of the individual cannot be altogether divorced from the welfare of the economy to which he belongs; and while *some* individuals can behave in a manner which maximises their own advantage but damages the common well-being, the greater the number of such persons the more their conduct will tend to be self-defeating. For example, by deciding to save a part of his income in the form of currency, an individual may under certain conditions reduce the total income of the community *pro tanto* and yet all the advantages of his saving may still accrue in full to him as an individual. On the other hand, if most recipients of incomes were suddenly to act in the same way simultaneously, all would personally suffer a probably more than counterbalancing disadvantage from the depressing effect upon the economy.[1]

It may not in the economic sphere be possible to go as far as Pericles[2] and say: 'Though a man flourishes as an individual, yet if his community is ruined, he comes to grief just the same, and is worse off

[1]See below, p. 111.
[2]Thucydides 2,60,3.

than if his own fortunes were bad while his country prospered'. Nevertheless there is a certain absurdity in describing as a good thing for the individual what is economically harmful to the community. Our answer to the question must be one which harmonises the interests of the individual and the community.

On the way, however, from the individual to the community we must look at saving by corporate bodies.

2. *Corporate saving*

The ultimate destination of company[1] savings, i.e. of undistributed net profits, is to be laid out in adding to the business assets of the company, by increasing its working or fixed capital or the purchase of additional goodwill.

They may be so laid out in the period in which the profits accrue. Alternatively, they may be held in the form of cash, securities or other assets for a shorter or longer period until what is judged to be the right opportunity arises for 'ploughing back'. Availability at the appropriate time will be the main criterion in determining the form in which company savings are held pending re-investment in the business; but to maintain, if not to increase, their real value will be an important secondary consideration, especially when inflation is apprehended.

It is a consequence of their purpose that company savings are liable to great fluctuation in the forms in which they are held or invested—from cash balances at the one extreme to embodiment in the company's fixed assets at the other. When a company's savings hitherto held in liquid form are 'ploughed back' into the business, the effect is to increase the monetary claim exerted upon the total production of the community. This increase may be relatively sudden in incidence and large in quantity if similar influences are affecting company decisions generally.

The effect may be intensified by the fact that provision out of profits for replacement of capital consumed—though by definition not saving, being related to gross not net income—is commonly held and treated in a similar manner to true company savings.

---

[1]Corporate savings are here discussed in the special, but infinitely the most important, case of *company* savings. The same general principles apply to the savings of all other corporate bodies, *mutatis mutandis*.

The amount of company saving is determined by the relative strength of opposing tendencies. On the one hand it is limited by the natural desire of shareholders to maximise their dividends and thus their personal income, and by the need of a company to distribute sufficient dividends to be able to attract any funds which it may sooner or later wish to raise from the public. Moreover, insofar as the Stock Exchange valuation of a company's shares tends to be influenced more by current and prospective dividends than by a history of 'ploughed back' profits, company saving carried to excess may expose the board to a take-over bid, i.e. to the risk of being displaced because existing shareholders are offered a price which corresponds more nearly than the Stock Exchange quotation to the true value of the company's assets.

On the other hand the inducements to maximise company saving are strong. Retained profits are an 'easy' form of capital for expansion. Unlike borrowing, by loan or debenture, no interest has to be paid on them: they avoid increasing the company's gearing, i.e. the proportion of prior claims upon profits. Unlike new equity, they do not require a favourable opportunity nor the public canvassing of the company's prospects and plans, nor is the balance of control liable to be altered. The board have the employment of retained profits very much in their own discretion. The prospective return may privately be estimated—with more or less sophistication and attention to 'discounted cash flow'—but if that should compare unfavourably with the return on existing capital employed or with the return being earned by capital elsewhere, or if the estimate is in the event proved ill-founded, few will be the wiser.

There are other factors which favour company saving. Boards and, it is believed, investors dislike dividends which fluctuate wildly between one year and the next: a steady, or steadily improving, dividend is what is aimed at. This means that boards will try to pitch distributions at a figure which can be met even in lean years, with the result that from this cause alone a substantial balance of company saving will occur, taking one year with another.

Political prejudice against high dividends is a further influence that cannot be ignored. 'Dividend restraint' has been commended by Conservative as well as Labour administrations as the counterpart or condition of 'wage restraint'. In discussion of incomes policy from 1961 onwards, profits have been put in the same bracket as wages; and popularly it is distributed profits which are understood by the term 'profits' and which attract unfavourable notice in certain quarters, especially when expressed as a percentage of nominal capital.

The propensity of companies to save is further reinforced by fiscal influences of two kinds: the treatment of income and of capital gains in the hands of shareholders, and the treatment of distributed and of undistributed profits of companies.

High rates of taxation of incomes have given shareholders a motive for preferring to receive profits in the form of an appreciation of their holdings, which can eventually be realised, if desired, in a capital form. To the wealthier shareholder an additional one or two per cent of dividend has little attraction compared with the increase in his wealth achieved by even moderately successful 'ploughing back'. This remains true even after the Finance Act 1965, because the rates at which capital gains are taxed under that Act are substantially lower than the higher rates of surtax.

Between 1947 and 1958, profits distributed were taxed in the United Kingdom at a higher rate than those retained; and though, to prevent tax avoidance, a contingent liability to tax at the higher rate remained attached to the profits retained,[1] the incentive to retention was appreciable. The differential rates were fixed initially at 25 per cent and 10 per cent respectively, but subsequently the difference was widened and the rates stood at 30 per cent and 3 per cent in 1958, when the difference was abolished altogether.

The argument for differentiation was demolished by the Royal Commission on Taxation[2] in words which deserve quotation:

"The mere retention of profits cannot be rated as an economic advantage: on the contrary it would better serve the public interest that a company should be encouraged to distribute those profits which it cannot put to fruitful use, in order that there may be a chance that they may be invested effectively elsewhere. Nor is it advantageous for the economy that the level of dividends should be kept down. Whatever other considerations bear upon the problem, the market value of shares in individual and commercial enterprises is depressed and an obstacle placed in the way of raising new capital."

[1] I.e. the difference between the lower and higher rates became payable if they were later distributed.
[2] Cmd. 9474 (1955), secs. 535-6.

The Minority Report, though rejecting a uniform profits tax unless accompanied by taxation of capital gains,[1] was equally out-
spoken:

> "Beyond a certain point the retention of profits by com-
> panies does not in itself stimulate the rate of capital formation
> —as is shown by the fact that in the last few years the net amounts
> retained by companies have greatly exceeded their financial
> requirements, both on account of capital expenditure and of
> investment in working capital. It can be argued that the system
> of financing capital expenditure so largely out of the undistributed
> profits of companies does not ensure the best use of the com-
> munity's savings. It makes it more difficult for fast-expanding
> firms to raise funds in the capital market; it strengthens the
> monopolistic tendencies in the economy; and it encourages
> wasteful expenditure on behalf of those firms who have more
> money than they can use and who are yet prevented (by custom
> and tradition as well as by the instruments of public control)
> from channelling these funds to their most profitable potential
> use."

In accordance with this view, the object of the single rate of profits
tax restored in 1958 was, in the words of the then Chancellor of the
Exchequer,[2] to 'improve the supply of capital to firms which need it
most'. The single rate was raised from 10 per cent to $12\frac{1}{2}$ per cent in
1960, and to 15 per cent in 1961; but in 1965 a major change in company taxation reintroduced fiscal discrimination on a substantial scale
between distributed and undistributed profits. Before the Finance Act,
1965, all profits, distributed or not, bore profits tax and income tax at
the standard rate. Since the application of that Act, corporation tax is
levied on profits, whether distributed or not, whereas income tax is
paid only by the recipients of distributed profits. Thus, distributed
profits bear both corporation and income tax, whereas undistributed
profits bear corporation tax only. Consequently more profit before
tax has to be made in order to put the same dividend after tax into the
hands of the shareholder. This is bound to reinforce powerfully the
other factors favouring retention of profits, and this was a motive
explicitly avowed by the Chancellor of the Exchequer: 'it gives a strong

[1]Ibid, p. 387.
[2]*Hansard*, 15 April, 1958, coln. 65.

incentive to all companies to plough back more of their profits for expansion'.[1]

Some idea of the magnitude of company savings, i.e. the undistributed net profits of companies, in recent years will be gained from Table II.

TABLE II
COMPANY SAVINGS: 1953 to 1964
£ million

Year	1 Gross income[2]	2 Dividend and interest payments	3 Undistributed income after taxation[3]	4 Column 3 as %age of Column 1
1953	3,379	754	1,307	39
1954	3,694	814	1,468	40
1955	4,093	911	1,800	44
1956	4,316	992	1,838	43
1957	4,591	1,074	1,965	43
1958	4,616	1,137	1,950	42
1959	4,961	1,238	2,205	44
1960	5,461	1,464	2,289	42
1961	5,439	1,672	2,246	41
1962	5,535	1,733	2,272	40
1963	5,997	1,823	2,500	42
1964	6,726	2,080	2,755	41

Source: *National Income and Expenditure* 1965.

Profits for Inland Revenue purposes are larger than true net profits, since (for example) they allow for replacement only on a historic basis. Nevertheless, the high and stable proportion of profits retained is striking.

Every year in this decade and the last, company savings, as calculated for national income purposes, though much lower than the undistributed profits of companies for tax purposes, substantially exceeded their investment in fixed capital, stocks and work in progress, so that there was an annual increase in their financial assets, taking all companies together. This is illustrated in Table III on the next page. Of course, the totals conceal wide variations between individual companies, many of which obtained considerable external finance for their investment.

[1]*Hansard*, 6 April, 1965, coln. 255.
[2]Includes gross trading income, rent and non-trading income, and income from abroad.
[3]Before providing for depreciation and stock appreciation.

TABLE III

COMPANY SAVINGS AND INVESTMENT: 1951 to 1964

£ million

	1951	1952	1953	1954	1955	1956	1957
1. Fixed investment by companies	627	634	675	792	969	1,211	1,390
2. Addition to stocks less stock appreciation	425	—63	65	200	352	234	184
3. Total of column 1 and column 2	1,052	571	740	992	1,321	1,445	1,574
4. Company savings[1]	1,403	1,225	1,307	1,468	1,800	1,838	1,965
Excess of 4 over 3	351	654	567	476	479	393	391

	1958	1959	1960	1961	1962	1963	1964
1. Fixed investment by companies	1,434	1,501	1,692	1,933	1,936	1,932	2,232
2. Addition to stocks, less stock appreciation	61	130	565	267	44	158	434
3. Total of column 1 and column 2	1,495	1,631	2,257	2,200	1,980	2,090	2,666
4. Company savings[1]	1,950	2,205	2,289	2,246	2,272	2,500	2,755
Excess of 4 over 3	455	574	32	46	292	410	89

Source: *National Income and Expenditure* 1965.

[1]As calculated for national income purposes.

Is company saving a good thing? Viewed from the standpoint of the ideal employment of the community's resources, a high degree of retention of profits by companies must be regarded with considerable reserve. The tests and standards applied to the investment of these retained profits are almost certain to be different from and less stringent than those applied to other investment. It follows that relatively more is re-invested directly, and relatively less is invested after passing through the medium of distribution, than would be ideal, with the consequence, *inter alia*, that the size of established firms may tend to exceed the economic optimum. A further possible disadvantage is the liquid position which may be built up out of retained profits not yet re-invested and which may contribute substantially to fluctuations in the relationship between demand and capacity.

Businesses will inevitably finance expansion partly out of their own savings; and in an expanding business it would be unrealistic to demand or expect anything approaching full distribution of profits.

On the other hand, any factor which strengthens the inherent bias towards retention must be unfavourable in its economic effect. In a free economy the *onus* of justification ought to be on company savings, not on distributed profits.

3. *Community saving*

We turn now to consider the utility of saving in the context of the community.

It may be conceded at once that saving in the form of an increase in reserves of gold and foreign currency is desirable only as long as those reserves remain less than adequate in relation to liabilities. Their essential function is to diminish variations, either in the exchange value of the community's currency despite temporary fluctuations in demand for it, or in the relative level of its imports and exports despite temporary fluctuations in international prices and trade. Beyond the point at which reserves are adequate to do this job, saving in this form not only confers no benefit but reduces the income available for consumption or for other kinds of saving, and tends to limit international trade.

Next, is saving through an increase in the indebtedness of other communities—lending abroad—a good thing? Such an increase may be deliberately willed on moral, humanitarian, political or strategic, rather than economic, grounds. Of this kind are loans made to other countries for fear of their going Communist, or to raise the standard of living in 'the underdeveloped parts of the world'. It would probably be correct to regard these as saving only in part or not at all, but rather as consumption for community purposes, like the testing of H-bombs or the maintenance of embassies in foreign capitals.

Where, however, the criterion and the motive is economic, the increase of indebtedness ought to 'pay', that is, it ought to be of such an amount that the last £1 of such indebtedness is expected to yield as great economic benefit as £1 consumed or saved in any other way, subject to the qualification that from the point of view of the community, though not of the individual, the return on external investment has to be compared net of the return on internal investment. The Finance Act, 1965 attempted to bring about that comparison. The question of external indebtedness therefore becomes part of the general question of the amount and direction of the community's saving, which we are about to discuss.

So far as stocks are concerned, there is an optimum level related to any given circumstances of supply and distribution and (in the case of raw materials and work in progress) to any given circumstances of manufacture also. To save by increasing stocks above that level is desirable only if those circumstances are to undergo a temporary variation, as for instance through an anticipated strike or hold-up of overseas supplies. Increase in stocks will confer economic benefit if it counteracts temporary fluctuations in supply and demand: if a Joseph will tell us the lean years in advance, stocking up during the fat years will be an advantage. On the other hand, if the increase in stocks is due to anticipation of changes in the value of money or to a misappreciation of future changes in supply and demand, it is a disadvantage and may cause or accentuate fluctuations in activity instead of tending to counteract them.

There remains community saving in its usual sense, that of devoting productive resources to supplying future rather than current satisfaction, particularly by increasing fixed capital. Community saving in this sense is a good thing if, but only if, it is of the 'right' kinds and the 'right' amount; and 'right' in this context means giving the greatest possible total satisfaction, so that if a different amount were saved, or if it were saved in other ways, the total satisfaction gained would be reduced. The expression 'total satisfaction' includes both current and future satisfaction, duly discounted in the case of the latter for deferment and uncertainty.[1]

So far the answer is a truism; but we get beyond truism the moment we ask: 'Whose satisfaction?' and 'Upon whose assessment?' Where it is my income that is being laid out, the answer to these questions is plainly 'mine'. Where it is the community's total effort which is being applied, the answer is further to seek.

To the second question, which we will take first, there are only two possible replies: the assessment must be either the government's or that of the community expressing itself by some spontaneous means. If the assessment is to be the government's, it follows that *all* the decisions which determine substantially how the community's effort is applied must be taken by the government. With control over the whole of production, the government can determine what part of it is

[1] Where part of the income consists—as it does in an open economy like Britain's—of goods and services obtained by exchange with other communities, the 'right' saving must include the amounts and kinds which are 'right' for meeting the purposes of exchange.

C

saved and in what ways. By assuming control of only part of the total production, however, it can do no such thing; for its decisions to increase or reduce saving may be counteracted by the decisions of individuals in relation to the part of production which remains outside its control. Thus the actual pattern of saving will merely be an accidental resultant of the interaction of the government's decisions with those of the community at large.

The alternative to assessment by the government is the method which corresponds to what we understand by a 'free economy' or 'free society'. The market mechanism by which the community spontaneously assesses satisfaction may be less than ideally efficient; but if this alternative is adopted at all, the efficiency of the assessment must be presumed to be diminished by the introduction of government decisions. No logical limits can be set to its application until we come to fields where such assessment is either impracticable or inherently impossible or deliberately renounced, and where the decision must therefore be governmental. For instance, there is no spontaneous means by which the community can compare the satisfaction of having £10 million more of fine new prisons with that of having £10 million more of fine new factories; the two satisfactions are not commensurable. Again, while there is no inherent impossibility in spontaneously assessing the satisfaction of having £10 million worth of fine new public highways against a like investment in factories, the practical difficulties of setting up the market mechanism—e.g. roads provided by profit-making companies—may rule it out. Thus, even in a free economy part of the community's income will be arbitrarily pre-empted (as it were) and assigned by the government to purposes which lie outside the reach of the community's spontaneous assessment of satisfaction.[1]

It would therefore be convenient to view the community's income in a free economy as divided not into two main categories—consumed and saved—but three: (a) income applied by government decision to purposes non-economic or otherwise not accessible to spontaneous assessment; (b) income otherwise consumed; and (c) income otherwise saved. This avoids putting expenditure on prisons and state schools

[1]The boundary line may vary somewhat from one period or society to another. The French word *vespasienne*, meaning a public urinal, is a reminder that the satisfaction yielded by a given investment in this type of convenience lay in imperial Rome within the limits of spontaneous community assessment—much to the profit of Vespasian, before his elevation to the purple.

in the same category of 'public investment' with modernisation of the nationalised railways or erection of nuclear power stations. Not that the 'pre-empted' portion of the community's income can be forgotten in studying the rest of consumption and saving. For one thing, its size has a direct, and may have a decisive, influence on the remainder. This is a topic to which we shall have to return later. Nor, because two satisfactions are incommensurable, are they without relevance to one another: we *do* try to relate the advantages of more and better prisons or schools or soldiers to those of more and better factories; the point is that in the nature of things we can do so only by government decision, and therefore arbitrarily and not spontaneously.

In a free economy, then, outside category (a) the 'right' amounts and kinds of saving are determined by an assessment of maximum satisfaction which is the spontaneous resultant of a process of community self-expression. Before, however, coming to look at that process of self-expression, let us try to answer the previous question: 'Whose satisfaction ?'

Where the assessment is the government's, the answer must be 'that of the community as a whole *as conceived by the government*'; elsewhere, it must, in a free economy, be 'that of the community as a whole *as expressed by it spontaneously*'. Now, the 'satisfaction of the community as a whole' which appears in either answer can only be a figurative expression,[1] because satisfaction is by its nature individual, personal and subjective. But different realities lurk behind the figure in the two cases.

Where the government decides, individual minds—often, perhaps, one individual mind—must attempt a synthesis of the satisfactions of the individuals making up the community. The attempt implies forming an intuitive picture of the community as an entity with an individual personality and thus with the capability of satisfaction. What is more, by conceiving that entity as surviving through several human generations, a synthesis is attempted of the satisfactions of individuals not only in the present, but in future generations. The synthetic entity is likely to be in the image of its maker. It would be strange if the order of satisfaction and values attributed to 'the community as a whole' did not bear a family resemblance to those

---

[1] It is in fact precisely the figure known to literary criticism (since Ruskin) as 'the pathetic fallacy', that is, the attribution of sense and feeling to that which by nature cannot possess them.

entertained by the rulers in their own persons, whether they sit in the Kremlin or on the Treasury Bench.

The same figurative expression, 'satisfaction of the community as a whole', conceals a different animal in the context of spontaneous self-expression by the community. Here it is a resultant, the resultant of the attempts of all the individuals in the community to maximise their satisfactions. It is not a composite total arrived at by adding together the satisfaction of all the individuals, still less a deliberate synthesis or reconciliation; it is simply a resultant of forces, the outcome of the private choices of individuals acting upon one another in the immensely complicated interrelationship which we call collectively 'the market'. The word 'outcome' is colourless: no moral, aesthetic or other perfection is claimed for it. By reason of the process of interaction itself and the inefficiencies of the market, it may well be a tardy, inadequate and distorted expression of those personal choices. Yet *some* expression it does provide of the wishes, values and expectations of the individuals who make up the community; and the expression is an objective one, at least in the sense that conscious interpretation and construction have no part in it. The alternative, be it remembered, is not some system of greater theoretical perfection and precision, but a series of decisions made and imposed by a government.

Let us now try to describe this mechanism which in a free economy determines the distribution, as between consumption and saving, of the resources not pre-empted by the government. The principle which underlies it is that the marginal return to resources in all their uses must always be tending towards equality: resources will not in the long run be applied to meeting current consumption which can be more advantageously employed in increasing the stock of houses or machinery. How then is relative advantage decided? The answer is arrived at by comparing the balance of supply and demand in one case and in the other. But supply of, and demand, for, what?

All production is undertaken to meet a prospective demand for consumption. There must always be some interval, however brief, between a decision to produce and the completion of consumption of the end product. But this interval is usually longer where the product is durable consumption goods, or where it is in turn to be the means of further production. The decision, for example, to produce a machine-tool implies an estimate of the demand for the products of the tool or for the products of the products of the tool over a substantial period, commencing perhaps some time ahead. The decision to build a block of flats to let depends upon an estimate of the demand for them over a period of many years starting with the date of first occupation.[1]

From the prospective demand is deduced, with the aid of further estimates and assumptions, a prospective profit in the sense of the margin whereby the price at which the goods or services can be sold exceeds their total costs. This profit, however, can only be earned if those having command of the requisite resources are willing to defer the use of that command for present enjoyment during the requisite length of time. The reward or gain which is obtainable for this deferment, to offset the inferiority of future compared with present enjoyment, may be expressed as a percentage, or rate of interest, on the value of the resources.[2] The profit anticipated must exceed this rate of interest by a margin sufficient to reward whatever exertion of enterprise is involved; otherwise the operation will not be undertaken.

Thus the distribution of effort between alternative forms of production is determined by two factors:

(a) expectations of demand at future periods of time, i.e. anticipated rates of profit; and

(b) the current charge for 'waiting' those periods of time, i.e. prevailing rates of interest.

If the current charge for 'waiting' is high, relatively less production will, upon the whole, be of a 'saving' character, and more will be of a 'consumption' character. In other words, the amount and direction of saving from the community's standpoint is determined by a generalisation of individual views of relative future profitability, interacting with a generalisation of individual views of the disadvantage of 'waiting'.

Naturally, any statement is over-simplified which disregards the lapse of time between decision and production: the actual employment of the resources of a community at any moment and the make-up of its output over any period is the outcome of earlier decisions, spreading backward over a considerable stretch of time, all of which are in

---

[1] I say "block of flats" rather than "house" and ignore the recent practice of building flats for sale, because where accommodation is bought in bulk in advance by the consumer (owner-occupation) the factor of anticipation of future rental values, though in fact still present, is overlaid and obscured by other considerations.

[2] See *Note* at end of Chapter.

continuous process of modification and replacement by others.

The relationship may be represented in a simplified form by the following diagram:

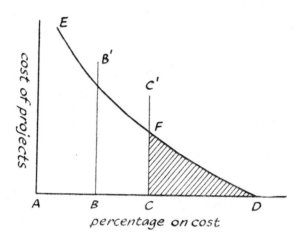

The line BB' marks the prevailing rate of interest (AB) for a given amount of 'waiting'; the line CC' includes the additional reward (BC) required for enterprise; and the curve DE represents the rates of profit anticipated on various projects which involve that amount of 'waiting'. The shaded area CDF is then the total value of the projects which will be undertaken. If the prevailing rate of interest were lower (or higher), the lines BB' and CC' would be farther to the left (or right) and—other things being equal—more (or fewer) projects would be undertaken. If the expectations of profit were lower (or higher), then the curve DE would similarly be farther to the left (or right) and fewer (or more) projects would be undertaken.

Since the resources actually provided are by definition equal to the resources actually used, the prevailing rate of interest may be regarded as that at which resources offering and resources demanded are equal, and the diagram may be redrawn as under.

The proposition may then be re-stated thus: for any given schedule of expected profit, if the propensity to 'wait' increases (i.e. if the curve AG becomes steeper), interest rates will fall—and more projects will be undertaken; if it diminishes (i.e. if the curve AG becomes flatter),

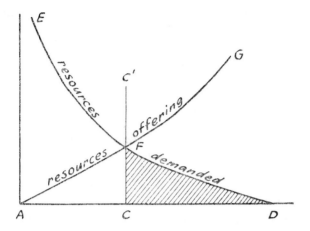

interest rates will rise—and fewer projects will be undertaken.

To say that the prevailing rate of interest represents the point at which supply and demand for resources for purposes which involve 'waiting' balance—in other words, their price—is not to say that the two curves are necessarily of the same shape. One may be much more 'curved' than the other. For example, the amount of resources offering may be comparatively inelastic in the face of variations in the demand. The rate of interest, however, will still express the balance between an assessment of future profitability and as assessment of the disadvantage of 'waiting'.

Let us now consider what value may be attributed to these two determinants of community saving in a free economy.

The individual views of relative future profitability, which are thus generalised, are attempts to assess the future demands of consumers, i.e. the demands for final economic satisfaction. Projection of present trends, or rather of the trends of the recent past, must inevitably play a big part in this. Unless there are obvious signs of approaching saturation, a rising consumer demand for a commodity or service will therefore usually tend to stimulate the provision of additional means of meeting it.

It is true that present trends may prove misleading if they suddenly cease or are reversed for reasons unforeseen. The other determinants of profitability, such as relative costs, may likewise be wrongly fore-cast, also perhaps on the basis of present trends. Both the general atmosphere of expectations (business confidence) and individual 'hunches' may be, and often are, disappointed. For all these reasons effort may be wasted which, with hindsight, we see could have been better applied.

On the other hand, it may be questioned whether a better assess-ment could be achieved by any other method than that of thousands upon thousands of individual intelligences directed, under the spur of reward and the penalty of loss, to appreciating how the future will grow out of a present which is part and parcel of their own experience. The errors of one group are as likely to offset as to magnify those of another: in an atmosphere of optimism, there is a premium on making allowance for over-optimism, while a prevalence of over-caution automatically creates the opportunities of boldness.

The object aimed at, economic satisfaction, is in the last resort a subjective thing. How is it likely to be more accurately predicted than by observing and endeavouring to anticipate the self-expression of the consumer? As a matter of recent experience in Great Britain, future demand has not been conspicuously better anticipated by industries which, being nationalised, were insulated from the inter-play of individual views of future profitability and obliged to rely upon the alternative method of centralised forecasting and decision.

The second factor, the current charge for 'waiting', to wit, the rate of interest which money lent for various terms and upon various securities commands, has been the subject of an immense amount of controversy.

The very attempt to equate the marginal return to resources employed over all the possible directions of employment would be impossible without some means of measuring the disadvantage of 'waiting'. A rate of interest, or rather a spectrum of rates of interest, is indispensable for the purpose.

If the equation were ever attained, it would be disturbed again the moment the community's assessment of the disadvantage of 'waiting' altered: if interest rates rose, fewer capital projects would qualify for inclusion in the new pattern of employment of resources; if they fell, more would qualify. This is not the same as saying that in the former case all or any of the resources thrown out of the production of fixed capital would be added to those engaged in other production, nor that in the latter case the additional resources devoted to the production of fixed capital would be deducted, in whole or part, from those engaged in current production. There might be a second consequence: the total amount of resources which were employed might also fall or rise.

Can the same virtues be claimed for the second as for the first of the two factors which determine the level of community saving in a free economy—for the generalised view of the disadvantage of 'waiting', as for the generalised view of future demand? The consideration that, if the disadvantage of 'waiting' had not been estimated so highly, more resources, particularly human resources, might have been employed, has caused many who approve the first factor without reservation to be sceptical about the second.

The gravamen is that if interest rates are 'too high' the community may fail to employ its resources 'fully' and thus also to distribute its employment of them 'rightly'. In practice labour is treated as the limiting factor determining when employment of resources is 'full', and the argument is that the community may fail to employ its manpower 'fully' if the generalised valuation of 'waiting' pushes the rates of interest 'too high'. Stated positively, the contention is that the rate should not be allowed to rise above the point at which all available labour is demanded.

There is no difficulty about this contention, apart from difficulties of definition ('all available labour,' etc.), provided it is recognised as being inconsistent with a free economy; for it can only mean entrusting assessment of economic advantage to the government, with power to give effect to that assessment by overriding the spontaneous expression of preferences through the market.

That spontaneous expression may also be overridden or set aside on grounds which are non-economic: the distribution of the community's resources between consumption and saving may be taken out of the economic sphere altogether. It is perfectly possible, for example, to say on political grounds (nationalism, patriotism, etc.) that a community ought to accept today satisfactions which it values lower instead of others which it values higher, in order that the nation may have arrived in five, twenty or fifty years' time at predetermined stages of industrial development. It is equally possible to say on moral grounds that this generation 'which now is', ought to be ready deliberately to sacrifice itself for the benefit of generations yet unborn

—provided the preacher is prepared to specify which future generation is to be exempt from this moral obligation and why.

But as long as the criterion remains economic, assessment of profitability and the interest rate are the only mechanism by which in a free society the individual aspirations to economic satisfaction, through saving or consumption, and all the accumulative and acquisitive instincts of individuals, can be reconciled within the potentialities of the community, so that the employment of its resources is in some sense the resultant and expression of all those impulses.

4. *Forced saving and personal saving*

It is scarcely possible to imagine a society in which the government would influence neither personal nor corporate nor community saving, that is neither the proportion of income which each individual refrains from consuming, nor the proportion of income which each corporation refrains from distributing, nor the proportion of the community's total productive effort which does not provide for current consumption.

In practice the very existence of government involves some influence on saving. By *taxation* for its purposes, the government reduces the disposable incomes of individuals and corporations and thus affects their ability to save and therefore presumably their propensity to save. This general effect must vary according to the particular ways in which the government raises taxation. By *expenditure* upon its purposes, the government determines in what proportions that part of the community's effort shall be devoted to current and to future consumption. This cannot avoid having effects on the way in which the residue of the community's productive effort is applied.

These consequences of taxation and government expenditure are as inseparable from the existence of government as the taxation and expenditure themselves; but there may be others. If the government *borrows* for its purposes, as well as taxing, it enters the market and bids for personal and corporate savings. This in turn affects the prices which they command, and so influences from yet another direction the pattern of the community's effort.

Again, if the government meets the cost of some of its purposes by creating money, then, to the extent that this raises the general level of prices and reduces the disposable real income of individuals and corporations, it produces similar consequences to increased taxation, and probably others as well, because it enhances the attractiveness of some applications of savings (viz. where they may be expected to retain their real value) and reduces that of others.

Thus the influence of government on savings ranges from a theoretical minimum, where government expenditure is nil, to a theoretical maximum, where the government directly disposes of the entire income of the community. In this matter, as in others, the theoretical minimum is not posed as a desirable aim but simply as a limiting case in relation to which the tendency and effect of a given change in government policy and behaviour can be judged and valued. For example, we can say that the lower the proportion of government outlay to national income, the more closely will the pattern and volume of saving approximate to those of a theoretical free society. We can also say that, given a certain government outlay, the less the government finances it by borrowing or creating money, the less the departure from that pattern and volume will be.

On the other hand, until one gets fairly near to the theoretical maximum, at which the government disposes of the entire national income, it is an error to suppose that it can determine either the total of the community's saving or the pattern in which that saving is laid out.

The government can raise a given amount by taxation or borrowing from the public and spend it, for example, on capital equipment for nationalised mines or railways; but it cannot be assumed that the amount in question is a net addition to savings. If the sum which the government collected in taxes or borrowed had been that much less, the savings of individuals or corporate bodies would almost certainly have been greater, though possibly not that much greater. Only if the national income were so low, or the government's share in it so great already, that no saving by the public was taking place, could the 'saving' achieved by the government be regarded as net. It is not even justifiable to assume that less would necessarily have been laid out on capital equipment for nationalised industries if they had been in private ownership: spontaneous saving might (for all we know) have flowed in the same directions.

Similarly, if the investment in the nationalised mines or railways is financed by the creation of new money, there is no assurance that other saving will not be reduced in proportion, or more or less than in proportion, as prices rise and enforce reductions in the total which the public saves or consumes. Only where the resources applied to the production of that mining or railway capital would otherwise have remained unemployed can we conclude that the government has brought about a net and specific addition to saving.

It is therefore misleading, in anything approaching a free economy, to describe government expenditure upon purposes other than current consumption as 'forced saving' if the phrase is intended to imply saving that would not otherwise have been done. All that can be asserted generally is that the government's action has affected in an arbitrary and unascertainable manner the application and (possibly) the amount of the community's total saving.

The virtues of a free and of a controlled economy, in this as in other spheres, are mutually destructive, so that logic points towards the fullest possible realisation of one system or the other. Any benefits from conscious government determination of the amount and application of saving can only be reaped at a very highly developed stage of control. Equally, if the free and spontaneous determination of the amount and application of saving has advantages, it is unwise to diminish them by any avoidable distortion, especially if the direction and degree of that distortion cannot be predicted or measured.

In a free society, therefore, it will not be primarily the pattern of government expenditure nor in the long run, for reasons already given (p. 28 ff.), corporate saving, but the saving of individuals— personal saving—which determines the disposition of the community's resources between consumption and saving, and the application of its saving. Accordingly, in what follows, the volume of personal saving in recent years in Britain is reviewed in relation to the national income and to the share of it laid out by the central government and other public authorities with powers of taxation. This is followed by an examination of the channels into which this personal saving has flowed, of the influences under which it has done so, and of the possible economic effects.

NOTE (p. 37)

THE RATE OF INTEREST AND LIQUIDITY

A refinement upon the notion of surrendering the present use or enjoyment of resources is the idea of surrendering the ability to use or enjoy them *at short notice*, which the individual retains if he saves in the form of money (currency) or in the form of assets unconditionally convertible into a known quantity of money or in proportion as the term for which he gives up control over them is shorter rather than longer.

Thus a rate of interest represents not only a reward for surrendering present use or enjoyment but also a reward for surrendering the ability to use or enjoy resources at short notice, i.e. liquidity. Where liquidity is absolute, the rate of interest is nil. As liquidity falls, the rate of interest (other things being equal) tends to rise.

The distinction between the two aspects of the rate of interest—as a measure of preference for present over future benefit and a measure of preference for liquidity—is not of practical importance. A rise in the rate of interest, which increases the reward for 'waiting', also increases the penalty on holding savings in a liquid form; and conversely, a fall in the rate, which reduces the incentive to 'wait', also reduces the cost of remaining liquid. It is difficult to imagine that reward in the shape of interest influences the decision to offer resources for investment but not the decision to refrain from applying them to consumption.

In the foregoing discussion, therefore, for simplicity's sake, the function of interest in relation to 'waiting' has been treated as subsuming its function in relation to liquidity.

Part II

Channels of personal saving

CHAPTER III

ASSESSING THE VOLUME

The total volume of personal saving cannot be at all precisely determined.

In recent years British governments have found it possible to estimate the annual total of gross personal incomes. From this may be deducted the sums paid by the recipients by way of tax on incomes and similar payments, such as national insurance contributions. From the net figure thus obtained can then be subtracted an estimate of the total expended by individuals on consumption. The residual figure may be regarded as representing the total of personal saving. Table IV reproduces the official estimate of this residual figure for 1938 and each of the last seventeen years, and shows the proportion which it has borne to total net personal incomes.

The equation of this residual figure with total personal saving is subject to substantial qualifications. The estimate of personal consumption expenditure includes, for instance, the element of saving represented by the value of consumption goods which survives at the end of the period, while on the other hand the income figure is not reduced by any provision for depreciation. These, however, are matters of definition. What is more serious is that errors in the income and consumption figures, so far as they do not offset one another, are included in the residual figures. The estimates of personal consumption expenditure are far from exact, and are subject to substantial revision. For example, the 1959 Blue Book increased the previous estimate for 1948 by £45 million, thus reducing the residual figure by over one-third, from £128 to £85 million. Subsequent revision reduced it further to a mere £19 million and then raised it again to £67 million. The estimates of total personal income are also subject to some, though less, revision.

49

Moreover, the stated margin of error or balancing figure in the estimates of national income and expenditure as a whole is consider-

TABLE IV

TOTAL PERSONAL SAVING: 1938 and 1948 to 1964

Year	Gross personal incomes	Tax[1]	Column 2 as %age of column 1	Net personal incomes	Column 4 less personal consumption	Column 5 as %age of column 4
	1	2	3	4	5	6
1938	5,078	420	8·3	4,658	264	5·6
1948	10,013	1,331	13·3	8,682	67	0·8
1949	10,572	1,457	13·8	9,115	140	1·5
1950	11,047	1,462	13·2	9,585	118	1·2
1951	12,002	1,654	13·8	10,348	124	1·2
1952	12,815	1,639	12·8	11,176	399	3·6
1953	13,595	1,668	12·3	11,927	443	3·7
1954	14,375	1,801	12·5	12,574	404	3·2
1955	15,622	1,959	12·5	13,663	552	4·0
1956	16,794	2,114	12·6	14,680	851	5·8
1957	17,701	2,259	12·8	15,442	854	5·5
1958	18,659	2,605	14·0	16,054	681	4·2
1959	19,747	2,688	13·6	17,059	889	5·2
1960	21,178	2,999	14·2	18,179	1,208	6·6
1961	22,897	3,321	14·5	19,576	1,705	8·7
1962	24,122	3,635	15·1	20,487	1,595	7·8
1963	25,500	3,833	15·0	21,667	1,644	7·6
1964	27,394	4,188	15·3	23,206	1,872	8·1

[1]I.e. payments of, and provision for, tax on income, plus national insurance and health service contributions.

Source: *National Income and Expenditure*, 1965.

able.[1] There is no means of knowing what part of the error relates to the estimates of personal income and consumption and thus vitiates the figures for deduced personal saving; but in many years the total error is

[1]The figure is subject to extensive variation, due to re-estimation of the underlying magnitudes. The 1959 Blue Book, for instance, made revisions which resulted in altering the error for 1957 from *minus* £68 million to *plus* £57 million and in the 1965 Blue Book the figure appears as *plus* £275 million.

large in relation to the personal saving figure. In 1948 the error was £61 million, compared with personal saving estimated at £67 million. This is an extreme case; but in 1954, when personal saving was an estimated £404 million, the error was £128 million.

The same risk of error dogs the alternative method of calculating personal savings,[1] by taking the estimated gross expenditure on fixed assets, stocks and work in progress and deducting from it the amount met out of taxation or out of corporate savings. The remainder (after allowance for external transactions), having come from personal incomes, may be reckoned to be the amount of personal saving. Once again, however, there is no means of knowing what part of the admitted margin of error is attributable to the various elements which enter into this calculation.

Theoretically it would be possible to check the residual figure for personal saving by comparing it with direct estimates of the net increase in personal assets, since all personal saving must be reflected in a growth either of physical or of financial assets. This method was explored by Mr. C. T. Saunders in a paper read to the Manchester Statistical Society in November 1954,[2] which concluded that it could not be regarded as successful. In particular, the movement of personal holdings of securities of all kinds cannot at present be identified and measured, nor can personal holdings of cash or the net indebtedness of the personal sector to the other sectors of the economy. This makes it impossible to build up a satisfactory aggregate of personal saving in all the various forms, which could then be used to check the residual figure. The behaviour of some of these assets, however, will be studied in detail in later pages of this book.

Even less secure is the attempt to estimate the change in the assets of the personal sector by grossing up samples, such as those provided by the estates annually becoming liable to estate duty or by surveys of the manner in which personal incomes are laid out.[3]

It remains therefore to take the residual figure as providing the best available indication of the order of magnitude and the movement of the total of personal saving, subject to the qualifications

[1] C.f. Blue Book 1965, Table 6.
[2] *Some Problems in the Estimation of Personal Savings and Investment.*
[3] E.g., H. F. Lydall, *British Incomes and Savings*, Oxford, 1955, pp. 109.

and caveats entered above. On this basis, the percentage of net personal income saved in each of the last seventeen years is plotted on Chart A. The behaviour of this percentage can be compared with the movement of various factors which, it has been suggested, may have a determining influence on propensity to save.

The continuous rise throughout the period in total personal and national real income no doubt facilitated the increase in personal saving; but it is clearly impossible to explain the behaviour of personal savings merely from the more or less steadily rising national real income.

The proportion of personal incomes paid in direct tax and compulsory contributions has remained remarkably steady throughout the period, varying only between a maximum of 15.3 per cent in 1964 and a minimum of 12.3 per cent in 1953. Between 1949 and 1954 there may be some trace of an inverse relationship between the weight of direct taxation and the proportion of personal incomes saved. Saving rose to two successive higher plateaux, in 1956-59 and 1960-64, although there was a marked upward trend in taxation throughout the decade. A minor dip in the savings figure, in 1958, happens to coincide with a temporary peak in taxation; but the peak of saving in 1961 was consistent with a continued increase in taxation. If there has in fact been any causal relationship between taxation and saving in this period, it could be explained by suggesting that as long as the margin of income felt to be available for saving was very small, variations in the incidence of tax were capable of producing a perceptible effect upon it. Since 1954, however, with steadily increasing net real incomes, the propensity to save has been governed by other forces though the tax burden also continued to increase, especially after 1957.

On the other hand there appears to be a more substantial correlation between the proportion of personal income saved and the long-term rate of interest as indicated by the average annual yield on Old Consols.[1] Only once in the period, namely, in 1957 — 59,

---

[1] Old Consols are admittedly not a perfect indicator of "the long term rate of interest". Nor, indeed, is any other stock: see the powerful critique in an article entitled 'Estimating the long-term rate of interest' in *The Times*, 17th November, 1959. The effect, however, of taking the average yield on British Government long-dated securities is not appreciably different.

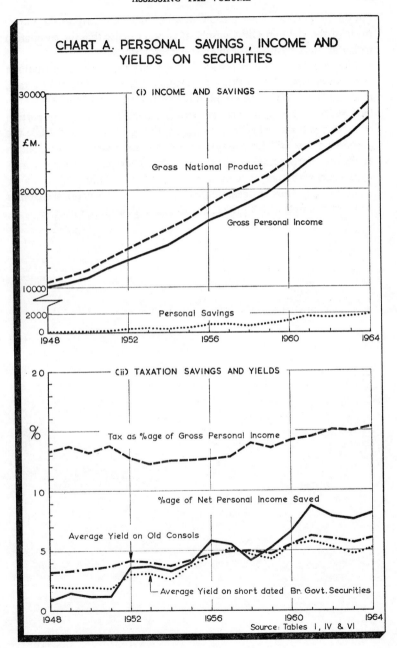

CHART A. PERSONAL SAVINGS, INCOME AND YIELDS ON SECURITIES

(i) INCOME AND SAVINGS

£M.

Gross National Product

Gross Personal Income

Personal Savings

(ii) TAXATION SAVINGS AND YIELDS

%

Tax as %age of Gross Personal Income

%age of Net Personal Income Saved

Average Yield on Old Consols

Average Yield on short dated Br. Govt. Securities

Source: Tables I, IV & VI

did the proportion of net income saved behave inversely to the movement of the yield on Old Consols. It is noteworthy that the correlation with the short-term rate of interest is even stronger.

The utmost caution is obviously necessary in attributing anything of a causal character to these correlations. At this stage, at any rate, it would be justifiable to say no more than this, that in the last seventeen years of increasing national and personal income the proportion of net income saved has also increased, though not evenly. While the proportion was still low, it appears to have been sensitive to changes in the tax burden; subsequently, its movement has had more correspondence with that of interest rates. Further enlightenment can be expected only from an examination in detail of the various channels into and through which private savings have flowed.

CHAPTER IV

MORTGAGE AND HIRE PURCHASE

1. *House mortgage*

There are two aspects of saving through loans on the security of houses: saving by the lender and saving by the borrower.

Take a simple case where a building society advances the cost of a house to a mortgagor. If the house is a new one, the savings of the shareholders and depositors of the building society are, in effect, applied to pay the wages, etc., of all the persons who contributed to produce the house, including the materials entering into it. If the house is an existing one, the savings have been transferred to and through the vendor into uses which it is impossible to identify.

Thereafter the mortgagor repays the loan with interest by instalments, normally out of his income. If the house were used up at the end of the mortgage period, he would have done no saving by this method over the period of repayment taken as a whole; for the outlay represented by the instalments would have been matched by consumption. Of course, in the normal case, the house still has a substantial life when the mortgage is paid off, and then the mortgagor has saved that part of the instalments which represents the value of the house at the end of the mortgage period. From his personal point of view the saving involved in each instalment payment is the acquisition of a further piece of unencumbered title to the house as at the end of the period. What actually happens, however, is that the equivalent value of that piece of title, having been saved by him, is transferred to the mortgagees. The economic effect depends on how they apply it, which may be either to the production or purchase of further houses or to other purposes altogether.

Thus if a house is worth £3,000 when erected and £2,000 when the mortgage is paid off, then (ignoring any alteration in values in the meantime) we start the period with assets of £3,000 and end it with assets of £5,000, i.e. a £2,000 house and £3,000 repaid to the mortgagees. The difference represents the saving which has been done by the mortgagor.

Saving done by way of mortgage repayment is contractual, and it can therefore be argued that it might not be done, or not to the same extent, if the saver had not bound himself at the outset by an obligation. On the other hand, when the mortgagee is a building society, the application of the savings is virtually predetermined: they will be re-lent for house purchase. Insofar, therefore, as money invested in building societies tends to be 'sticky' and remain so invested, the probable consequence is a higher outlay of savings on the erection, or through the purchase, of dwelling-houses for owner-occupation than would be the case if house mortgage were not institutionalised; for if the whole of the funds lent by societies had to be directly attracted in the form of new shares and deposits (instead of less than half as in fact), it seems certain that a considerably higher rate of interest would have to be offered by mortgagors. At this higher rate the total borrowed by mortgagors, and thus the total of savings laid out on dwelling-houses for owner-occupation, would probably have been less than it has actually been. This does not apply, or not to the same extent, to mortgages outside the building society system.

The amount of gross saving through building societies each year is the sum of the capital repayments which are made to them and of the new share-money and deposits they receive. The net saving is not so easy to determine; for it is that amount diminished not only by the withdrawals of shareholders and depositors but also by the reduction of other assets of their investors and the depreciation of mortgaged properties. In practice, however, it is simplest to ignore these latter qualifications and study the figures of net increases in shares and deposits and of capital repayments. These are shown in the first two columns of the following Table.

TABLE V

SAVING THROUGH BUILDING SOCIETIES: 1922 to 1965

£ million

Year	Net increase in shares and deposits	Repayments (principal only)	Column 1 as %age of total personal savings (Table IV)	Gross personal expenditure on new houses (less land)	Gross advances by societies	Advances net of repayments (columns 5-2)
	1	2	3	4	5	6
1922	12	15			23	8
1923	17	17			32	15
1924	19	20			41	21
1925	23	24			50	26
1926	23	27			52	25
1927	28	29			56	27
1928	43	29	not available		70	41
1929	43	34			75	41
1930	57	41			89	48
1931	46	46			90	44
1932	49	54			82	28
1933	29	68			103	35
1934	51	72			125	53
1935	43	78			131	53
1936	47	83		145	140	57
1937	52	87		132	137	50
1938	43	87	16	125	137	50
1939-1945			not available			
1946	50	121	19	49	188	67
1947	72	150	69	64	243	93
1948	78	161	116	45	264	103
1949	98	161	70	54	276	115
1950	110	164	93	50	270	106
1951	97	169	78	58	268	99
1952	119	160	30	99	266	106
1953	157	167	35	167	300	133
1954	216	196	53	221	373	177
1955	192	216	35	260	394	178
1956	154	208	18	289	335	127
1957	171	220	20	296	374	154
1958	193	228	28	314	375	147
1959	270	289	30	382	517	228
1960	206	319	17	466	560	241
1961	202	323	12	520	546	223
1962	372	345	23	522	613	268
1963	495	432	30	541	849	417
1964	516	503	28	674	1,057	554
1965	658	510			963	453

Sources: Radice, *Savings in Great Britain 1925-1935*, Oxford, 1939; *National Income and Expenditure*; Saunders (see p. 51); *Building Societies Year Book*; Reports of Chief Registrar of Friendly Societies; *Annual Abstract of Statistics; Financial Statistics.*

The Table discloses a number of notable features. As would be expected, given the rapid and continuous increase in the total number of owner-occupied houses throughout most of the period, saving by repayment mounts more or less steadily in money terms. It has nearly always exceeded the net increase in shares and deposits: the only exceptions have been, in the inter-war period, the slump years 1928-1931, and in the post-war period, the single year 1954, and the years 1962-64. However, it must be remembered that the repayment figures exaggerate the amount of net saving for two reasons: first, because (as already mentioned) they exclude depreciation; secondly, because a considerable proportion of repayments—it has been estimated in some years at as high as 50 per cent[1]—are technical repayments upon transfer of a house from one mortgagor to another.

On the other hand, not only the amount of saving by building society share and deposit, but its ratio to total personal saving fluctuate widely. Since 1951 it has averaged about 27 per cent, with a high point of 53 per cent in 1954 and troughs of 19-21 per cent and 16-12 per cent in 1956-57 and 1960-61 respectively.

No great significance attaches to the precise percentage figures, because of the insecurity of the estimates of total personal saving. There is also a minor disturbing factor, in that a small fraction of the deposits and shares of building societies (chiefly the deposits) are corporate assets.[2] However, the general trend is clear beyond dispute: building society shares and deposits were the most significant channel for personal savings in the post-war years 1947-51. Thereafter they lost this pre-eminence, but have accounted, with substantial fluctuations, for very roughly one-quarter of personal savings.

Columns (4) and (5) of Table V provide some indication of the direction in which the total savings through building societies, represented by repayments *plus* the net increases in shares and deposits, have been laid out. By comparing gross personal expenditure on new houses with the gross advances of the societies, we see that, whereas in the years before 1939 the two figures varied little from one another, the experience since 1945 has been quite different. Up to 1951 advances averaged five times the expenditure on new houses. Thereafter the ratio fell rapidly; but in the last five years, 1960-64, taking a 'lean'

[1]Lydall, l.c., p. 118.
[2]Deposits are only about a tenth of shares and fluctuate within comparatively narrow limits; and since the war it is probably only between 1952 and 1955 that there may have been appreciable corporate investment in deposits.

with a 'fat' period, the figures for advances are still running about 28 per cent above those for new houses.

Once again, the two columns are not perfectly commensurable, because not all the advances by building societies are on houses, while a substantial part of total personal expenditure on new houses is met by liquidation of other personal assets, by direct personal savings of the current period, or by loans from sources other than building societies. Moreover, part of the cost of land excluded from the figures in column (4) represents payment for development work (in the form of roads and other services). What is nevertheless clear is that a substantial part of the amount of the advances, probably not less than one-fifth and possibly much more, is laid out (however that may be) *via* transactions in existing houses.

A further important comparison is that between the inflow into the building societies, by way of net increases in shares and deposits *plus* repayments, and the outflow from them, by way of advances (columns (1), (2) and (5).) Before 1950 the outflow substantially exceeded the inflow; in 1950-52 the two drew level; after 1952 the inflow moved ahead. Total inflow in the seven years 1953-59 was £2,869 million, total outflow £2,662 million; total inflow in the five years 1960-64 was £3,707 million, total outflow £3,619 million. This means that whereas in the years immediately after the war the societies were liquidating assets, since 1952 they have been increasing them, that is, they have been channelling part of the savings which pass through them into the purchase of trustee securities.

To form some notion of the causes which determine the proportion of personal savings channelled through building societies, we may inquire how the yield which they offer is related to the movement of interest rates generally. Table VI shows the rates of share interest recommended by the Building Societies Association, both net and grossed up for income tax at the standard rate, side by side with the yield on 2½ per cent Consols, and expresses the excess of the former over the latter as a percentage.

On the basis of Table VI, Chart B compares changes in the proportion of savings channelled through the societies since 1948 with the interest advantage which they offer for a shareholder paying income tax at the standard rate. The comparison cannot be exact, for several

TABLE VI

YIELDS: BUILDING SOCIETY SHARES AND
OLD CONSOLS: 1946 to 1964

per cent

Year	Average yield on 2½% Consols	Building society shares: average interest		%age excess of column 3 over column 1
		net	grossed-up for standard rate income tax	
	1	2	3	4
1946	2·60	2·15	3·91	50
1947	2·76	2·15	3·91	42
1948	3·21	2·16	3·93	22
1949	3·30	2·15	3·91	18
1950	3·54	2·21	4·02	14
1951	3·78	2·22	4·19	11
1952	4·23	2·38	4·53	7
1953	4·08	2·45	4·51	11
1954	3·75	2·45	4·45	19
1955	4·17	2·61	4·59	10
1956	4·73	3·08	5·36	13
1957	4·98	3·45	6·00	20
1958	4·98	3·48	6·05	21
1959	4·82	3·34	5·69	18
1960	5·42	3·37	5·50	1
1961	6·20	3·54	5·78	—7
1962	5·98	3·70	6·04	1
1963	5·58	3·56	5·81	4
1964	6·03	3·50	5·71	—5

Sources: *Building Societies Year Book*; *Annual Abstract of Statistics*; *Report of Chief Registrar of Friendly Societies*.

reasons: the choice of the yield on Old Consols is only a rough and arbitrary guide to the rates open to savers in alternative investments; the recommended rates of interest are not followed by the whole of the building society movement; the attractiveness of building society interest to the income tax-payer at the standard rate is greater than to others and not by any means all shareholders are in the former class.

Nevertheless it is obvious that in the nine years to 1955 there was a close correlation between the proportion of personal savings which the societies attracted and the relative superiority of the yield which they offered. In only one year, 1950, did the two trends diverge. The *Economist*[1] was right, under the title 'Lessons of 1955', to say:

[1]Supplement, *Building Societies and Housing*, 5th May, 1956.

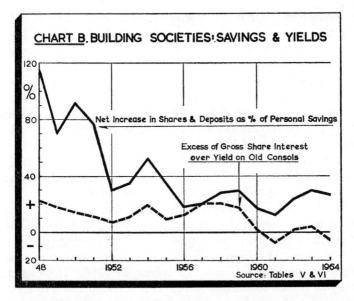

CHART B. BUILDING SOCIETIES: SAVINGS & YIELDS

Net Increase in Shares & Deposits as % of Personal Savings

Excess of Gross Share Interest over Yield on Old Consols

Source: Tables V & VI

"The societies have learned that they must adapt themselves to the current rate of interest. The old theory that the money came from a special class of small saver who would never try to use it elsewhere to better advantage has been blown sky high." The correlation was broken in 1956, when the proportion of personal savings going into building society shares and deposits fell in a year when the relative attractiveness of building society interest increased. After 1956 the correlation returns, though it does not become marked again till 1959-60, and this time at a lower level. There is probably more than one explanation for this. One certainly is the special favour accorded since 1956 to national savings (see p. 84 ff.), which over-trumped the building societies. A second is probably the sharp increase amongst savers, especially since 1955-56, in consciousness of the consequences of inflation, which has reduced the attraction of non-appreciating forms of savings such as building society shares and deposits.

2. *Other mortgages*

Mortgages, other than on dwelling-houses, fall into two categories: loans (usually to businesses and other corporate bodies) secured on commercial property, and loans to local authorities secured on the local rates.

In this case, saving by the borrowers, i.e. by way of repayment, involves no significant element of *personal* saving. The residual asset which a company acquires by paying off a mortgage on its property represents corporate saving. The mortgage debt incurred by a local authority is paid off out of the yield of local and national taxation and of charges for services (such as house rents or water rates); but in any case the assets of local authorities are normally amortised over periods which correspond broadly with their anticipated useful life.

On the other hand, in saving by the lenders a considerable element of personal saving may be directly or indirectly involved.

Satisfactory figures on either kind of mortgage are hard to come by. As regards commercial mortgages, it is known that the life funds of insurance companies are a considerable source—£82 million net in 1956, and £53 million in 1957—while the contribution of super-annuation funds is negligible (£2 million in 1957).[1] However, the sum total of such commercial mortgages does not appear to be known, though a rough estimate can be made from the yield of Stamp Duty. Stamp Duty on mortgages of 'lands and houses'—the term 'houses' includes all buildings and not only dwelling houses—yielded[2] £2.2 million in 1956-57, £2.2 million in 1957-58 and £3.7 million in 1963-64. At ¼ per cent these yields imply total advances on mortgage amounting to approximately £880 million, £880 million and £1,480 million respectively. After deducting the amounts advanced on house property —£335 million to £1,059 million through building societies[3] and perhaps a third as much again from other sources—it appears that mortgages on commercial lands and buildings were running in these three years at approximately £220 million per annum. What portion of this sum goes to new development and what part is transferred to other destinations by existing property or sites changing hands, there is no means of determining; but it seems clear that appreciable quantities of corporate and personal savings are channelled through commercial mortgages to the creation of new non-residential buildings.

Information on local government borrowing has until recently been scanty. It is known that the net annual borrowings of local

[1] *Radcliffe Report*, paras. 248, 253.
[2] Annual Reports of the Commissioners of Inland Revenue.
[3] See Table V.

authorities in Great Britain from the public, otherwise than by the
sale of stocks, increased as follows in the eight years 1951-58:[1]

	£ million		£ million
1951	22	1955	49
1952	55	1956	330
1953	139	1957	351
1954	193	1958	376

These borrowings appear to have been fairly evenly divided between
borrowing on mortgage and 'temporary borrowing', i.e. by way of
overdraft or loan without security. Thus, the outstanding mortgages
of local authorities increased by £377 million in the three years 1955-56
to 1957-58 and their temporary borrowings by £342 million.[2] Temporary borrowings, however, other than those in anticipation of
revenue (which are excluded from the foregoing figures), are sooner
or later replaced by formal loans, of which, again, the greater part will
presumably be on mortgage.

Apart from direct investment by individuals and companies, and
by trusts and other investment agencies, for which local authority
mortgages provide a convenient and profitable application of temporarily liquid funds, two important sources of supply for local authority borrowing are superannuation and pension funds, and the special
investment departments of the Trustee Savings Banks. Superannuation and pension funds, for instance, invested £16 million net in
local authority mortgages in 1957, while outstanding advances to
local authorities by the special investment departments have recently
increased as follows:[3]

	£ million		£ million
1956	46.6	1960	22.1
1957	28.2	1961	32.4
1958	7.4	1962	61.0
1959	17.5	1963	72.6
			———
			£287.0 million
			———

More detailed information in a somewhat different form has become
available from 1961 onwards in the series shown in Table VII below.

[1] *Radcliffe Report*, p. 33, Table 5.
[2] Ibid., p. 358, Table 38.
[3] *Annual Reports of the Trustee Savings Banks Inspection Committee.*

TABLE VII

LOCAL AUTHORITY NET BORROWING

Year	Quoted securities	Central government	Other public corporations	Banks[1]	Other financial institutions[2]	Loans and mortgages				Total
						Industrial and commercial companies	Persons	Overseas residents	Others	
	1	2	3	4	5	6	7	8	9	10
1961	30	—20	—6	85	101	49	179	39	18	475
1962	138	—34	1	82	107	27	184	41	19	565
1963	87	—36	2	86	167	133	104	—3	61	607
1964	78	172	5	154	100	63	120	29	17	738
1965	220	435	2	5	279	—78	233	—25	—19	1,052

Source: *Financial Statistics.*

[1]Excluding bank overdrafts.

[2]Including borrowing from own superannuation funds.

This discloses (column 7) a substantial volume of direct personal savings flowing into local authority borrowing, in addition to any which are channelled through banks and other institutions or take the form of purchase of securities.

3. Hire Purchase[1]

There are two aspects of hire purchase[2] of durable consumer goods and of plant and equipment, as there are two aspects of borrowing on mortgage. The lender's savings are being channelled into the production of the commodities concerned. The borrower, insofar as he is in possession of a valuable asset when the debt is cleared, has done saving to that extent over the period of the hire purchase, and his savings in turn have been channelled to the production of more commodities or to other uses altogether.

In the absence of any means of estimating the residual value of hire-purchased assets, the absolute amount of saving done by borrowers in this form cannot be stated; but it may be assumed that, relatively speaking, if hire purchase debt rises, this form of saving will be rising also. None of it, however, features in the residual figure of personal saving (p. 49), which treats the purchase of durable consumer goods (other than houses) as wholly consumption of the year in question; nor does any of it appear in company saving, which represents the difference between distributed and total net profits.

If the total of the outstanding hire purchase debt remains constant, no net saving is being done by lenders through hire purchase. Net saving by lenders occurs only when the outstanding debt increases. As regards the borrowers (the hire purchasers), they are saving a constant *gross* sum annually if the outstanding debt remains constant—gross, that is, of the value of the assets consumed (the depreciation). However, the composition of the assets hire purchased is varying all the time, and if, in the process, their useful life is on average increasing, then *net* saving by hire purchasers is increasing—and *vice versa*. The static hire purchase debt is thus a revolving credit, by means of which —though not necessarily because of which—hire purchasers do a certain amount of saving.

[1]See generally Harris, Seldon and Naylor, *Hire Purchase in a Free Society*, IEA, 3rd ed., 1961.

[2]The expression is used to include credit sales, which differ from hire purchase in that ownership passes with the first and not with the last payment.

The following Table illustrates the manner in which hire purchase debt has increased since 1955—there are no statistics for earlier years.

TABLE VIII
HIRE PURCHASE DEBT: 1955 to 1964

At December	Total debt outstanding	Increase (decrease —) on the year	£ million Increase (decrease —) on the year in debt of persons
	1	2	3
1955	461		—
1956	376	−85	−63
1957	448	72	37
1958	556	108	82
1959	849	293	224
1960	935	86	22
1961	934	−1	−21
1962	887	−47	−1
1963	959	72	69
1964	1,115	156	109

Sources: *National Income and Expenditure*, 1965, *Board of Trade Journal*, 12 February, 1965 (figures for 1961-63 were revised in this issue following the 1961 Census of Distribution reports), *Annual Abstract of Statistics*, 1964, *Board of Trade Journal*, 21 August, 1959 for years 1955-56.

The amount of net saving by the personal sector which is involved on the borrowing side of hire purchase must be substantial, though far less than the gross saving. Without a reliable estimate of the average life of the hire purchased assets, it would be impossible to give a net figure. Perhaps it would not be unreasonable to guess that at least half of the hire purchase payments of individuals and households, now running at about £400-£500 million per annum, represents not contractual saving, analogous with insurance premiums, but contractual expenditure, analogous with rent.

On the lending side, the sources of hire purchase finance in 1957-58 were investigated by the Radcliffe Committee. They found that (para. 207) "while a large part of hire purchase credit is advanced by retailers and dealers, well over half comes directly or indirectly from the finance houses", and that (para. 209) "in 1958 the finance houses drew over half their funds (apart from capital and reserves) from the public (including industrial and commercial concerns) on deposit". The "industrial and commercial concerns" are indeed the principal depositors: at the end of 1957, out of over £90 million deposits, only

£10 million belonged to private individuals and a further £17 million to insurance companies "and other financial institutions" (para 210). It is therefore obvious that not more than a small fraction of the total increase in hire purchase debt represented saving of the private sector by way of loan, whether directly or indirectly. What was chiefly happening was that companies were employing their savings by placing them on deposit to finance hire purchase.

Recently another contributor to the financing of hire purchase—bank advances—has been growing in importance. It may confidently be assumed that this growth is not at an end, and that the virtually complete link-up between the larger hire purchase finance houses and the joint stock banks which occurred in 1958-9 will result in a larger rather than a smaller proportion of hire purchase finance being provided by bank advances. There is of course a further, indeterminate part of hire purchase finance provided from bank advances insofar as hire purchase operations by retailers, wholesalers and manufacturers are directly or indirectly financed by the banks. The advances by the banks to hire purchase finance houses have been as follows since separate statistics became available:[1]

£ million

	1954	1955	1956	1957	1958
Outstanding	15·1	38·6	28·7	31·4	32·0
Change on year		+23·5	−9·9	+2·7	+0·6

	1959	1960	1961	1962	1963
Outstanding	89·1	138·6	138·6	104·9	105·0
Change on year	+57·1	+39·5	—	−33·7	+ 0·1

The relationship between bank advances and saving is discussed below (p. 113); but it is fair to describe the situation on the lending side of hire purchase broadly as follows, that the banks, industry and commerce are maintaining a revolving pool of credit, which helps to sustain the trade in consumer durables, which expands as it expands and which helps it to expand. On the borrowing side hire purchase provides a vehicle for a certain amount of personal saving by the acquisition of durable assets which continue to yield satisfaction after the instalments have been completed.

[1] *Annual Abstract*, 1964, Table 350.

CHAPTER V

LIFE ASSURANCE AND SUPERANNUATION

Saving occurs where the recipient of an income refrains (or is restrained) from consuming a portion of it in consideration of future payments to be made to him or his on the occurrence of some eventuality. This is the case of saving through life assurance or superannuation.

Not all income set aside in the form of insurance premia or superannuation contributions represents saving. One part of such premia or contributions must be reckoned as consumption, the part namely which pays the expenses and profits of those who organise the operation. The remainder of a premium also ranks as consumption where the contingency insured against is loss or accident: such a premium is simply part of the cost of maintaining the insured asset intact, and is no more saving than the provision for repair or replacement of assets which wear out. Where, on the other hand, the contingency is death, retirement or the attainment of a specified age, then the object and effect of the insurance is to secure future consumption by oneself or others by deferring present consumption, and the net premia or contributions, after deduction of costs and insurer's profit, represent saving.

It will be convenient to dispose first of a special case, where by its nature the saving cannot be quantitatively expressed. That is where the portion of income thus saved is expressed in terms not of money but of an accrued right to the benefits.

This can happen where the government promises its servants a certain scale of superannuation but does not make deductions in respect of it from their salaries. Because of this promise it needs to pay its present servants less than it would have to if there were no non-contributory pensions. The result is that the state raises so much less in taxation to pay the salaries of its present servants but so much more to meet the superannuation of its past servants.[1]

Thus the state's present servants are, in effect, transferring part of their income (represented by the imputed value of their accrued superannuation rights) to the general taxpayer, by whom it is laid out as part of his net income, while the state's past servants receive *via* taxation part of the general taxpayer's gross income.

Where a firm promises an employee a non-contributory pension and does not itself take out an insurance in respect of it—the case, that is, of a 'non-funded' non-contributory scheme—the effect is similar but simpler: the firm's income is increased by the imputed value of the accrual of pension rights to its present employees and diminished by the cost of the current pensions of past employees. The net result may be negative or positive: where it is positive, i.e. a net increase in the firm's income, that extra amount is laid out along with the rest, being either distributed or retained.

It is hard to deny that the civil servant is 'saving' the annual accrual of his superannuation rights, just as much as the employee who re-mains in employment where contributory superannuation is compulsory is saving the amounts stopped out of his salary or wages *plus* any amounts contributed by his employers. This is made clear in the curious mongrel case of teachers' superannuation: a percentage deduction is made from the teacher's salary, but these deductions are simply used to reduce the current cost of the education service, which at the same time is increased by the cost of current superannuation payments.[2]

There being no estimate of the value of the annual accrual of super-annuation rights in 'non-funded' schemes, the national income statistics substitute the amount of the pensions and other benefits actually paid by the respective employers year by year. This *pis aller* inevitably vitiates the shape and movement of the figures; for there is no reason

[1] The amount of the balance, negative or positive, depends on the ratio between present and past servants and the value at which the present accrual of future superannuation rights is assessed.

[2] It is an anomaly, but an unavoidable one, that the teacher's contributions (though not, be it noted, any excess of the value of accrued superannuation rights over the amount of the contributions) are included under 'contributions of employees' in the *Blue Book's* Capital Account of the Private Sector, whereas the notional savings of those covered by non-contributory schemes are not.

why the two amounts should be equal or even approximate to equality. Moreover, an adjustment of the superannuation rates for past employees may raise the total of payments sharply without there being any comparable increase in the value of the rights accruing to existing employees in the same year. Finally, when 'non-funded' schemes are funded, there will be an alteration in the saving figures to which no real change corresponds. The Central Statistical Office[1] are therefore right in describing the procedure as 'unsatisfactory'.

Apart from the special case of 'non-funded' schemes discussed already the sums saved for superannuation, etc., are transferred by way of premia or contributions to an insurance company or other body (such as trustees) which undertakes to make the future payments in consideration of them. Where the person to whom the future payments are to be made is an employee, it is usual for the employer to pay part or the whole of these sums out of profits or other revenue, while the remainder (if any) is deducted from the employee's salary or wages. There is no means of ascertaining whether, if the employer's share of the contribution were not paid, the employee's salary or wages would have had to be increased by precisely the same amount; but for practical purposes it is simplest to make this assumption. The total contribution may then be regarded as saved by the employee out of an income in which the employer's share is included.

The gross totals annually paid, or assumed to be paid,[2] by way of premia or contributions in the last seventeen years are shown in column (1) of Table IX. Subject to deduction of administrative costs and profits, and to the very important caveat already entered in regard to assumed contributions, these figures may be taken as representing the sums annually saved through this channel.

In addition, part of the annual income from the invested funds must be regarded as personal saving, insofar as it represents the means of paying future benefits 'with profits'. The rest, after any distribution to shareholders of insurance companies, etc., is corporate saving. Subject however to this (not very important) qualification, the net increase [column (3)] in the funds attributable to superannuation, life assurance, etc., can be taken as net saving of the personal sector through this channel.

---

[1] *Sources and Methods*, 1956, p. 77.
[2] I.e., the amount of current benefits in the case of 'non-funded' schemes.

TABLE IX
SAVING THROUGH LIFE ASSURANCE AND
SUPERANNUATION: 1948 to 1964

Year	Paid (or assumed paid) by way of contributions, etc.	Column 1 as %age of net personal incomes (Table IV, col. 4)[1]	Net increase in relevant funds	Column 3 as %age of personal saving (Table IV, col. 5)
	£m		£m.	
	1	2	3	4
1948	496	5·7 (5·0)	218	325
1949	538	5·9 (5·1)	238	170
1950	589	6·0 (5·3)	270	229
1951	659	6·4 (5·5)	314	253
1952	707	6·3 (5·5)	351	80
1953	763	6·4 (5·6)	393	89
1954	813	6·5 (5·7)	437	108
1955	885	6·5 (5·7)	477	86
1956	963	6·6 (5·7)	514	60
1957	1,066	6·9 (6·0)	577	68
1958	1,159	7·2 (6·2)	646	95
1959	1,234	7·2 (6·2)	713	80
1960	1,338	7·4 (6·3)	812	67
1961	1,434	7·3 (6·3)	864	51
1962	1,552	7·6 (6·4)	936	59
1963	1,705	7·9 (6·7)	1,048	64
1964	1,818	7·8 (6·6)	1,132	60

[1]For figures in brackets see p. 72.
Source: *National Income and Expenditure*, 1965.

Two comparisons are instructive. One is to compare the gross sums annually saved by way of actual or assumed premia and contributions with the total of net personal income [column (4) of Table IV]. The proportion of net personal income thus applied has been relatively very steady, rising from 5.7 per cent in 1948 to 7.8 per cent in 1964. The rises between 1956 and 1958 and between 1961 and 1963 may have been exaggerated by pension increases (see above, p. 70); but the general picture of the personal sector devoting to superannuation a stable but slowly rising proportion of net income is probably accurate.

Broadly speaking, the contributions paid or assumed to be paid for superannuation purposes, and two-fifths of life assurance premia, are paid out of untaxed income; and the interest on superannuation funds is also exempt from tax. Therefore roughly three-quarters of the saving through these channels is done out of untaxed income. The policy underlying the relevant tax provisions is discussed elsewhere (p. 131 f.); but it follows that the more accurate comparison is between contributions, etc., and *gross* personal incomes (after payment of national insurance and health contributions). This comparison [shown in brackets in column (2) of the Table] gives a still more steady curve of increase, but does not otherwise alter the picture materially.

The second comparison is between the net increase in superannuation, etc., funds and the total saving of the personal sector [column (4) of the Table]. Until the big upswing in saving took place in 1952, the net increase in the funds was considerably larger than total personal saving through all channels; in other words, saving through this channel was partly offset by personal dis-saving. Even since the upswing of 1952, life assurance and superannuation have accounted for about half total personal saving, the proportion rising whenever total saving relapses, as it did in 1954, 1958, and 1962-63.

This is the behaviour which would be expected from a form of saving so largely outside the influence of individual decisions. In the case of employees, the commitment once entered into is nearly always binding or at least very difficult to throw off and the saving is largely or entirely unconscious. Elsewhere the process is contractual, and discontinuance or reduction of saving is opposed by strong considerations both of a prudential and a financial character. The fact that a steadily increasing percentage of income is devoted to these payments presumably reflects, among other causes, the steadily advancing diffusion of occupational and other pension schemes.

Where the sums saved for superannuation, etc., are funded, the body undertaking to make the relevant future payments uses the premia or contributions to purchase assets which it then holds as the means (along with any increment to those assets in the meanwhile) of meeting its future liabilities. Thus the income forgone by the savers goes to increase the total amount available for the purchase of bonds, equities and other suitable assets. When the liabilities come to be discharged, then in theory the assets are sold and their value has to be matched by an equivalent amount of savings then coming forward for their purchase, which amount is then transferred to the insured persons or superannuitants as income.

Again in theory, it would appear that a point is eventually reached when the purchases and sales, the positive and negative effects for saving, balance. In practice, this point of equilibrium lies at an indefinite distance. The continuing increase in the number of persons covered and in the amounts of premia and contributions, relatively to the number of current beneficiaries and the amounts of current benefits, has more than offset the rising proportion of the retired to those of working age. Consequently life assurance and superannuation funds have continued, and are continuing, to increase. Thus, looking at the process from the community's point of view, we can best consider the payments in and out as being offset against each other—a transfer of income from one set of individuals to another—with the surplus of payments in over payments out representing the net saving done through this medium. The picture is, of course, oversimplified to the extent that it leaves the annual income of the funds out of account.

The direction of so substantial a fraction of personal saving, that is, the character of the assets acquired and held against these liabilities, must be of considerable significance in the economy. A sufficiently accurate picture of that direction is given by Tables X(i) and X(ii) which show by percentages the types of assets held and purchased during 1956-57 and 1963-64 for the life funds of members of the British Insurance Association and for superannuation funds not reassured with life offices, both separately and together.

The omission from the Tables of the life funds of non-members of the British Insurance Association and of the pension funds of co-operative societies does not materially affect their significance. They show that well over half the savings flowing through these channels go to companies, and that a further fifth finds its way, *via* mortgages and real estate investments, preponderantly into industrial and commercial fixed capital. About one-sixth is transferred to the government.

Within these general magnitudes there are noteworthy variations, both between 1956-57 and 1963-64 and between the insurance companies on the one hand and the funds on the other. The insurance companies reduced their lending to the government much sooner than did the funds: in 1957 the former were investing only 7 per cent in gilt-edged against the latter's 20 per cent, whereas in 1964 the former's investment in gilt-edged was 24 per cent while the superannuation and pension funds were barely investing in gilt-edged at all. The propensity of the pension funds to invest in companies is noticeably greater than that of the insurance companies. The 'cult of the equity'

TABLE X (i)

ASSETS HELD AND ACQUIRED BY LIFE AND SUPERANNUATION FUNDS: 1956 and 1957

Type of Asset	Life Funds of members of British Insurance Association			Superannuation and pension funds		Total		Per cent (except col. 8)
	Held end 1957	Acquired in 1956	Acquired in 1957	Held end 1957	Acquired in 1957	Held end 1957	Acquired in 1957	(£m.)
	1	2	3	4	5	6	7	8
Mortgages	14·4	31·6	17·3	2	1	10·8	10·9	55
British Government and Government-guaranteed securities	27·6	1·2	7·3	34	20	29·6	12·3	62
Overseas public securities	2·0	−2·0	−0·8	3	1	2·4	—	—
Debentures and loan stocks	14·6	17·8	22·0	12	17	13·8	20·1	101
Preference stocks and shares	7·2	5·4	4·4	4	1	6·2	3·0	15
Ordinary shares	17·3	19·7	25·1	21	37	18·4	29·8	150
Real property and ground rents	9·6	11·2	12·6	3	5	7·5	9·6	48
Other investments	7·3	15·1	12·1	21	18	11·3	14·3	72
TOTAL	100·0	100·0	100·0	100	100	100·0	100·0	503

Sources: *Radcliffe Report*, Tables 15, 16; British Insurance Association.

TABLE X (ii)

ASSETS HELD AND ACQUIRED BY LIFE AND SUPERANNUATION FUNDS: 1963 and 1964

| Type of Asset | Life funds of members of British Insurance Association | | | | | | Superannuation and pension funds | | | | Total | | | |
| | Held end 1964 | | Acquired in 1963 | | Acquired in 1964 | | Held end 1964 | | Acquired in 1964 | | Held end 1964 | | Acquired in 1964 | |
	£m. 1	% 2	£m. 3	% 4	£m. 5	% 6	£m. 7	% 8	£m. 9	% 10	£m. 11	% 12	£m. 13	% 14
Mortgages … … …	1,372	17·2	92	15·8	248	16·1	53	1·8	1·8	0·8	1,425	13·0	249·8	14·4
British Government and Government-guaranteed securities	2,352	29·5	136	23·8	729	47·2	735	24·6	3·4	1·6	3,087	28·2	732·4	42·1
Overseas public securities	77	1·0	2	0·4	12	0·8	50	1·7	−4·1	−1·9	127	1·2	7·9	0·5
Debentures and loan stocks	1,240	15·6	145	25·2	227	14·7	452	15·2	41·3	19·5	1,692	15·5	268·3	15·4
Preference stocks and shares	364	4·6	22	3·8	25	1·6	75	2·5	1·6	0·7	439	4·0	26·6	1·5
Ordinary shares	1,731	21·7	119	20·6	233	15·1	1,421	47·6	133·3	62·9	3,152	28·8	366·3	21·1
Real estates and ground rents	795	10·0	60	10·4	70	4·5	198	6·6	34·7	16·4	1,021	9·3	86·7	5·0
Other investments	28	0·4	−1	—	1	—								
TOTAL	7,959	100·0	575	100·0	1,545	100·0	2,984	100·0	212·0	100·0	10,943	100·0	1,738·0	100·0

Source: *Board of Trade Journal*, 9 July, 1965
Note: In columns 1–6 values of British Government and Government-guaranteed securities are nominal values.

reached the pension funds later but took a stronger hold, whereas the insurance companies are more flexible in their policy and readier to take advantage of a prospect of quick appreciation by purchasing gilt-edged securities when interest rates are exceptionally high as in 1961-62.

Nevertheless, the role of life assurance and superannuation in financing companies is impressive. In the years 1957 and 1964 they channelled personal savings to the value of £250-300 million and £660 million respectively into stocks and shares. These figures are high in relation to the total capital raised by companies. In the same years the total value of new issues by United Kingdom public companies (excluding banking, insurance and finance) was about £309 million in each case.[1] There was therefore going on an appreciable net transfer of securities of public companies to these funds from other holders, so that substantial amounts of the savings were channelled to unidentifiable destinations through the hands of the previous owners of existing securities. The direct role of the funds in taking up new issues is large. In 1956, out of a total investment by life assurance funds alone of £111 million in company securities, nearly £70 million was subscribed to new issues.[2] Moreover, it may be assumed that part of the sums applied by the funds to the purchase of existing securities will also have ultimately flowed into new issues.

One cannot fail to be struck by the importance of the direct and probably also the indirect link between the investment financed by new issues of public companies and the large and steadily growing mass of savings which flows through the life assurance and superannuation funds. It is indeed not going too far to say that such investment is preponderantly financed through life assurance and superannuation.

From more than one point of view this close connection between saving through assurance or superannuation on the one hand and investment by industry and commerce on the other hand is healthy. It means that promises of future income are being secured in part upon the future production which present investment makes possible, just as part of the cost of present superannuation is met by the earnings on past investment. In part, however, and for much the greater part, future payments will depend upon future savings, as present payments are largely financed by present savings. For a long

[1] *Annual Abstract*, 1964, Table 355; and see p. 99.
[2] Evidence of the British Insurance Association to the Radcliffe Committee (*Evidence*, Vol. 2, p. 36).

time ahead, the balance between savings flowing in and payments flowing out will be positive. Theoretically, as the proportion of old people to active approaches its "normal" proportion, the volume of pension fund saving might diminish; and if we ever reach the point at which the population as a whole actually declines, it could become negative.

These theoretical considerations, however, are of little practical interest. The establishment of equilibrium, let alone an actual decline in population, has been pushed into an indefinitely remote future by the surge in birth-rate between 1956 and 1964, not to mention such factors as the continuing improvement in the expectation of life. Even if the population were in equilibrium or declining, there would probably still be a positive balance of savings, because as long as standards of living continued to rise, each generation would be likely to make more provision for age than its predecessors.

The need of the insurance companies and pension funds to find opportunities to invest a large and steady volume of savings is undoubtedly a stabilising factor in the capital market, tending to moderate the short-term fluctuations. A special instance of this function is the operation of the insurance companies as underwriters for over one-half of all new issues of equity and other industrial securities. As the Radcliffe Committee said (para. 247), "their willingness to hold the securities makes the issuing houses prefer the insurance companies to many other underwriters". Nor does it seem that this useful characteristic of these funds as investors is counterbalanced by any distorting effect; for apart from seeking to maintain—outside equities—a balance between the length of their assets and the length of their liabilities, it does not appear that the funds as investors are guided by any special criteria beyond those of commercial judgment and prudence, and wide variations in investment policy may be noted between one office and another.

This is perhaps the most appropriate context in which to refer to National Insurance, which for a brief period shortly after its inception contributed an infinitesimal compulsory quota to the amount of the national income borrowed by the Government from the public. National Insurance contributions are levies imposed on the gross profits of employers and the incomes of individuals. Where the total of these contributions exceeds the total of the corresponding benefits paid out, plus the cost of administration, any surplus is lent by the National Insurance Fund to the Government. As Table XI shows, this actually happened in three of the earlier years of the scheme (1949-1951), but has never recurred and presumably never will. Apart from those three years, the National Insurance benefits have been and are a heavy and increasing net charge upon the yield of general taxation. Thus the scheme is in effect simply a system of redistributing income, and its relevance to saving in any sense of the term is nil.

TABLE XI

NATIONAL INSURANCE CONTRIBUTIONS AND
BENEFITS: 1948 to 1964

£ million

Year	Contributions[1]	Benefits	Surplus
	1	2	3
1948	318	334	—16
1949	394	379	15
1950	399	389	10
1951	410	407	3
1952	435	474	—39
1953	484	527	—43
1954	491	531	—40
1955	552	614	—62
1956	601	670	—69
1957	631	702	—71
1958	760	912	—152
1959	784	987	—203
1960	795	992	—197
1961	930	1,125	—195
1962	1,034	1,213	—179
1963	1,138	1,413	—275
1964	1,275	1,497	—222

[1]Net of contributions in respect of the National Health Service (formed into a separate contribution in 1957).
Source: *National Income and Expenditure*, 1965, and previous issues.

CHAPTER VI

NATIONAL SAVINGS

The expression 'national savings', which originated in the First World War, is now used as a generic term for the following channels through which money is lent to the Government:

Trustee Savings Banks (ordinary departments)

Post Office Savings Bank

National Savings Certificates

Defence and National Development Bonds

Premium Savings Bonds

These channels of lending to the Government all have the further common characteristics that the sums which are allowed to be held or deposited in each by any one individual are limited to a relatively low figure, and that such sums can be withdrawn on demand or virtually so, with the minimum of formality. Both the interest and the principal are guaranteed (in money terms) by the state.

Apart from these common characteristics, the various forms of National Savings differ widely in nature, and their experiences, which are shown for the last sixteen years in Table XII, have also been widely divergent.

The figures given are the increases (decreases—) on the year in the amounts remaining invested at the end of each financial year. The amounts include accrued interest; for this also is income of the investors which is saved through National Savings, inasmuch as it is not withdrawn and laid out on consumption. Consequently, the variations are not identical with the net inflow (or outflow, as the case may be) of cash to (or from) the Exchequer.

TABLE XII NET ANNUAL NATIONAL SAVINGS

1949-50 to 1964-65

£ million

Financial Year	National Savings Certificates	Defence Bonds	Post Office Savings Bank	Trustee Savings Banks Ordinary Departments	Trustee Savings Banks Special Investment Depts.	Premium Savings Bonds	Total
	1	2	3	4		5	6
1949-50	9·4	−20·2	−12·7	49·1	(1·8)		25·6
1950-51	24·7	−21·4	−34·5	35·3	(1·8)		4·1
1951-52	42·4	−56·9	−53·7	24·2	(3·3)		−44·0
1952-53	36·9	−55·9	−70·2	−0·9	(7·7)		−82·4
1953-54	41·0	−38·1	−46·0	−8·6	(40·3)		−51·7
1954-55	67·4	23·0	−17·0	7·7	(40·9)		81·1
1955-56	31·7	−29·3	−34·6	−21·2	(45·7)		−53·4
1956-57	43·6	−34·8	1·0	6·7	(46·2)	66·4	82·9
1957-58	−40·2	−40·0	−24·9	13·9	(27·9)	81·3	−9·3
1958-59	108·7	107·9	−12·2	16·6	(28·0)	68·1	289·1
1959-60	73·8	145·4	40·5	39·6	(45·9)	37·5	336·8
1960-61	67·8	104·0	27·9	23·8	(55·6)	56·3	279·8
1961-62	1·0	16·1	25·5	15·3	(78·4)	42·1	100·0
1962-63	40·7	47·0	30·5	28·2	(110·5)	41·9	188·3
1963-64	17·3	19·6	30·5	44·5	(146·5)	43·6	155·5
1964-65	−2·6	−86·8 (166·9)[1]	14·2	39·1	(135·2)	54·2	185·0

Source: *Annual Abstract of Statistics*, 1959 to 1965.

[1] National Development Bonds, introduced on 15 May, 1964. They replaced Defence Bonds.

There is of course no reason to regard a net increase either in National Savings generally or in any particular form of National Savings as equivalent to income saved in the relevant period. The whole or part of any such increase may equally well represent the conversion of other assets into National Savings, and, as we shall see, this must in fact have happened widely. The economic effect will then depend on the nature of those other assets. For example, if they were marketable securities or real assets, the ultimate result may still have been a transfer to the Government of current income saved by an initial purchaser at the beginning of a sequence of purchases and sales. If, on the other hand, the increase in National Savings was matched by an outflow of cash from the Government itself, as for instance by the repayment of dated stock or post-war credits, no saving is involved.

A net *decrease* in National Savings always represents an outflow of cash from the Government; and this is met either by other borrowing, by taxation or by increasing the quantity of money. One of these methods, borrowing, may and usually does involve current saving.

Thus the relation of the movements of National Savings to saving by individuals or by the personal sector as a whole is inscrutable. This does not, however, mean that there is nothing to be learnt from a study of these movements in the context of personal savings generally.

In National Savings as a whole, there was practically no net increase or decrease over the nine-year period 1949-58. Net increases of over £80 million in some years were balanced by net decreases of the same order in other years, leaving, over the whole period, a net decrease amounting to about £47 million. In the seven years since 1957-58 there has been a massive increase amounting to about £1,450 million.

In this increase all forms of National Savings participated to some extent; but otherwise their experiences since 1949 have been a study in contrasts. National Savings Certificates have been steadily popular, with set-backs in 1957-58, 1961-62 and 1964-65, and a spurt in 1958-60. Defence Bonds and the Post Office Savings Bank, on the other hand, were heavy and persistent losers until 1958. Afterwards Defence Bonds participated in the 1958-60 upsurge, and the Bank has been a modest, steady gainer until 1964-65. The ordinary departments of the Trustee Savings Banks declined in popularity over the years to 1955-56, but then recovered and have shown gains even in the worst years.

F

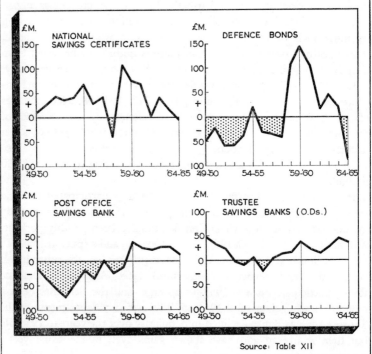

CHART C. NET ANNUAL NATIONAL SAVINGS

Source: Table XII

Finally, Premium Savings Bonds since their inception in 1956, have been a 'winner', averaging a steady million gain a year, even after the first flush of enthusiasm in 1956-58 had died away.

These divergencies can only be understood by studying the characteristics of the individual forms of National Savings against the background of the general movement of savings and of interest rates.

On Chart C are plotted the fortunes of the various forms of National Savings, and on Chart D a comparison between the movement of National Savings as a whole, personal saving as a whole, and the long-term rate of interest.

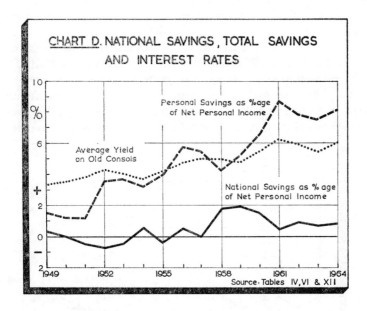

CHART D. NATIONAL SAVINGS, TOTAL SAVINGS AND INTEREST RATES

Personal Savings as %age of Net Personal Income

Average Yield on Old Consols

National Savings as %age of Net Personal Income

Source: Tables IV, VI & XII

What emerges clearly from this comparison of National Savings with total personal saving is that upon the whole their movements have been inverse. Another way of describing the phenomenon is to say that while total personal saving has tended to follow the general movement of rates of interest (see p. 52 ff.), National Savings have tended to vary inversely with it. The reasons for this inverse movement will appear as the individual forms of National Savings are studied separately.

1. *Savings banks*

The ordinary departments of the Trustee Savings Banks and the
Post Office Savings Bank are, respectively, the oldest and second
oldest forms of National Savings. They have this in common, that
they offer no more than 2½ per cent on deposits and have done so
without variation since the beginning of the century. The first £15
of this interest has been free of income tax, except for surtax payers,
since the Finance Act of 1956.

In practice, because tax is not deducted before interest is credited
or paid, the interest was worth its tax-free value for many taxpayers
until 1951, simply because these sums were widely omitted from
returns of income for tax purposes. In 1951, however, a provision[1]
was made under which any interest credited or paid gross by banks,
etc., including the Trustee Savings Banks and the Post Office, had
to be disclosed to the Inland Revenue on request. This resulted in
numerous assessments having to be made to recover underpayments
of tax. The sums involved were scarcely worth the administrative cost
and the friction with the public; and this was no doubt an important,
though naturally unspoken, reason for the step taken in 1956 to relieve

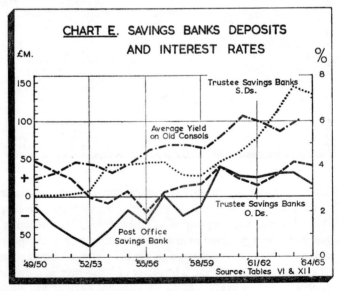

[1]Finance Act, 1951, sec. 27; re-enacted as Income Tax Act, 1952, sec. 29.

from income tax the interest on the first £600 deposited by non-surtax payers.

In the light of these facts it is interesting to compare, against the background of the ruling interest rate, the performance of the two institutions, both of which observe the same limit on deposits, viz. £5,000 per depositor (£3,000 before 1960, £2,000 before 1952).[1]

For the six years to 1955-56 inclusive the movement of deposits was inverse to that of the long-term rate of interest. In the case of the Post Office, which experienced a heavy net reduction in deposits throughout the period, this inverse correlation was remarkably precise; in that of the Trustee Savings Banks, which managed more or less to keep their heads above water until 1955-56, the correlation was slightly less exact, because the recovery in response to lower interest rates generally in 1953-55 was more sluggish.

In 1956-57, for the first time, deposits in the savings banks rose *with*, instead of *against*, the general interest rate. As that was also the year in which interest on the first £600 of an individual's deposit or deposits in these banks (£1,200 in the case of a married couple) was relieved of income tax, it looks as though there might be a causal connection; and if so, it would have to be concluded that many savings bank depositors are not only conscious of the movement of interest rates in general and quick to respond to it in their behaviour, but are also liable to income tax at or near the standard rate on their marginal income.

After the initial boost in 1956-57, deposits with the savings banks seem to have resumed their inverse relationship with the general interest rate, though the Trustee Savings Banks continued to experience increases in 1957-59.

The behaviour of the Trustee Savings Banks' ordinary departments cannot be fully understood without reference to that of their special investment departments, in which persons with at least £50 in the ordinary department may invest up to £3,000 (£2,000 before 1960, £1,000 before 1956) at rates of interest ranging, with different Banks, up to 2½ per cent above that obtainable in the ordinary departments. This money is invested in Government and local authority stocks, mortgages and certain other securities, as permitted by the National

[1]In addition, before 1960 there was a maximum of £500 in any one year.

Debt Office. These investments are in fact not part of National Savings but go towards the total amount of cash being offered in the mortgage and securities market.[1]

It seems probable that the inflow to the special investment departments after 1952-53[2] was the main factor which muted the response of deposits in the ordinary departments to variations in the general rate of interest. Indeed, it is known that large transfers from the ordinary to the special investment departments took place in these years. On the other hand, the link between the two departments may be one reason why the Trustee Savings Banks' experience fluctuated at a higher level than that of the Post Office throughout the period, and why they were able, unlike the Post Office, to avoid a net loss of deposits. Other reasons no doubt are the greater services to depositors, such as the cheque service now coming into operation, and the closer personal contact with them which the Trustee Savings Banks are able to maintain, and also the spread in recent years of factory and office schemes for deducting savings from wages and salaries and paying them directly into Trustee Savings Banks.

2. National Savings Certificates

The net annual increases in the value of National Savings Certificates, principal and interest together, were given in Table XII. The interest, however, though calculated as accruing from year to year, cannot be drawn unless and until the Certificates have been encashed. The interest element is therefore income of the holders of Certificates only in a very special sense and subject to the important qualification that the holders cannot realise it in the year concerned, whether they want to or not, unless they also realise the capital. While it may nevertheless be harmless to include the accrued interest on National Savings Certificates both in the total of personal income and in the total of personal savings (cf. p. 79), the experience of this form of National Savings can be usefully analysed only by looking at the movements of purchases and encashments. These movements are shown in Table XIII and plotted on Chart F.

[1]The intention to legislate to create a similar department of the Post Office Savings Bank was announced in the 1965 Budget (*Hansard*, 6 April, 1965, coln. 278).
[2]The annual net increases in the amounts invested in the special investment departments of the Trustee Savings Banks are shown on Chart E.

The interest earned on National Savings Certificates is so calculated as to increase more or less progressively with each succeeding year until maturity, so that the rate of interest earned by holding a Certificate to maturity is greater than if it is encashed previously. There is to that extent a penalty on premature encashment. For example, the interest on the Tenth Issue (August 1956) accrued at the following rates: 1st year, £2 4s. 5d. per cent; 2nd year, £2 3s. 6d.;[1] 3rd year, £3 3s. 10d.; 4th year, £4 2s. 6d.; 5th year, £3 19s. 2d.;[1] 6th year, £5 14s. 3d.; last year, £8 2s. 2d.

The interest on National Savings Certificates is tax free. Therefore for those liable to tax at substantial rates, the effective rate of interest can be very high. For example, the Tenth Issue, if held for the full seven years, yielded £4 3s. 11d. tax free, which was the equivalent of £7 6s. 0d.[2] to a standard rate income-tax payer, or £16 15s. 8d. to a surtax payer taxed at 15s. in the £ on his marginal income. The Table and Chart show the interest obtainable to maturity on the issue of Certificates which was on sale at any given time in the last seventeen years; it is shown both net and grossed up for income tax at the standard rate.

National Savings Certificates are thus an attractive investment for the income-tax payer at standard and higher rates who is willing to forgo use of the interest for a period of years. Over a period appreciable sums can be invested in National Savings Certificates; for example, Certificates of the four issues on sale in the last seventeen years could be purchased up to a total principal value of £3,050 (£500, £1,050, £900 and £600 respectively).

For the most part, as Chart F shows, the annual ratio of purchases to encashments of National Savings Certificates moved almost exactly as might be predicted from the relation between the general long-term interest rate and the grossed up interest on certificates. When the effective rate of interest on Certificates lagged behind rises in the general rate, as in 1949-50, 1955-56 or 1961-62, net purchases of Certificates declined. At other times, such as 1954-55 and 1956-57, when the gap widened to the advantage of National Savings Certificates, net purchases increased.

[1]The fluctuations are due to the fact that interest is expressed as increases of 4d., 6d., 8d., 10d., 1s. and 1s. 6d. in the value of a unit. When the increase is the same two years running, there is a fall in the percentage rate of interest in the second year of the pair.
[2]£6 17s. 0d. after April 1959.

TABLE XIII

NATIONAL SAVINGS CERTIFICATES: 1948/9 to 1964/65

Year	Purchases £m.	Encashments £m.	Difference £m.	Accrued interest £m.	Net Saving £m.	Interest on new units per £100 — Net	Interest on new units per £100 — Grossed up for standard rate of income tax
	1	2	3	4	5	6 £ s. d.	7 £ s. d.
1948–49	121·8	126·1	−4·3	26·5	22·2	2 13 2	4 16 8
1949–50	102·0	125·8	−23·8	33·2	9·4	2 13 2	4 16 8
1950–51	132·4	136·1	−3·7	28·4	24·7	2 13 2[1]	4 16 8[1]
1951–52	155·5	139·5	16·0	26·4	42·4	3 0 11	5 16 0
1952–53	160·8	138·0	22·9	14·0	36·9	3 0 11	5 16 0
1953–54	155·4	136·4	19·0	22·0	41·0	3 0 11	5 10 9
1954–55	182·8	136·8	46·0	21·4	67·4	3 0 11	5 10 9
1955–56	181·3	161·6	19·7	12·0	31·7	3 0 11	5 5 11
1956–57	335·2	261·1	74·1	−30·5	43·6	4 3 11[2]	7 5 11[2]
1957–58	211·7	231·8	−20·1	−20·1	−40·2	4 3 11	7 5 11
1958–59	358·4	228·2	130·2	−21·5	108·7	4 3 11	7 5 11
1959–60	244·3	177·8	66·5	7·3	73·8	4 3 11	6 17 0
1960–61	234·2	179·5	54·7	13·1	67·8	4 3 11	6 17 0
1961–62	173·9	190·0	−16·1	17·1	1·0	4 3 11	6 17 0
1962–63	179·1	167·9	11·2	29·5	40·7	4 3 11	6 17 0
1963–64	151·7	175·3	−23·6	40·9	17·3	3 15 9[3]	6 3 8[3]
1964–65	161·8	195·6	−33·8	31·2	−2·6	3 15 9	6 3 8

Source: *Annual Abstract of Statistics*, 1959 to 1965.
[1] £3 0s. 11d. and £5 10s. 9d. respectively in February-March, 1951.
[2] From 1 August, 1956.
[3] From 13 May, 1963.

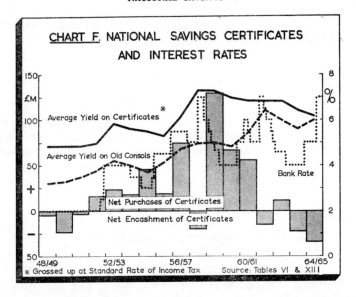

CHART F. NATIONAL SAVINGS CERTIFICATES AND INTEREST RATES

Average Yield on Certificates *

Average Yield on Old Consols

Bank Rate

Net Purchases of Certificates

Net Encashment of Certificates

48/49   52/53   56/57   60/61   64/65

* Grossed up at Standard Rate of Income Tax   Source: Tables VI & XIII

What is not explicable in terms of the general long-term interest rate is the behaviour of purchases and encashments in 1957-58, when the rise to a peak figure in 1958-59 was preceded by a plunge to the first net decrease in the amounted invested which had occurred for eight years. Yet the advantage of the effective rate of interest on Certificates over the general long-term rate was actually slightly greater in 1957-58 than in 1958-59, and in both years the standard rate income-tax payer could expect the high return of £7 6s. 0d. on his purchases of Certificates if held to maturity. What was unique, and unfavourable to National Savings Certificates, in 1957-58? There can scarcely be any doubt about the answer. It was the *short-term* interest rate.

In all three years, 1956-57 to 1958-59, as column (2) of Table XIII shows, there was heavy switching—at the rate of about £100 million a year over and above normal maturities and encashments—out of existing holdings of National Savings Certificates. In 1956-57 and 1958-59 these maturities and encashments were greatly exceeded by new purchases of the current Issue; but in 1957-58—a year of continued increase in total personal savings (p. 50)—the balance was the other way. The attraction of high short-term rates of interest proved irresistible to the class of purchaser who was buying Certificates heavily in 1956-57 and who resumed doing so again in 1958-59, stimulated perhaps by the expectation, not fulfilled until 1963,[1] of a new issue at lower yields.

The same phenomenon of an abrupt plunge into deficit marked the next 7 per cent Bank rate in 1961-62, but there was little recovery afterwards before the third 7 per cent in 1964-65.

Thus the experience of National Savings Certificates not only reinforces the deduction already reached that National Savings are sensitive to the prevailing long-term rate of interest, but shows that those whose decisions determine the balance of purchases and encashments are alive to short-term opportunities and prospects.

3. *Defence and National Development Bonds*

The experience of Defence and National Development Bonds, depicted on Chart G, presents a complementary picture.

There was a substantial net decrease in the holding of Defence Bonds in each of the nine years 1949-50 to 1957-58, except 1954-55. Until 1958-59 the rate of interest on the Bonds, paid half-yearly to the holder's bank or direct and liable for income tax, was always below the prevailing general long-term rate of interest.

There was a slight premium on retaining the Bonds, which were sold in £5 units, for a minimum period of years, and a slight penalty upon encashment at less than six months' notice; but otherwise the Bonds were an almost perfectly liquid investment. On the last, 5 per cent issue, for instance, there was a premium of £3 per £100 (tax free) on retention for seven years, and a penalty of £2 10s. 0d. per £100 on encashment at less than six months' notice. There was a limit on purchases of Bonds of any one issue—£5,000, for example, on the last issue[2]—but holdings of earlier issues could be converted into the current issue without regard to this limit. The Bonds could be repaid at the government's option until a minimum period—seven years in the case of the last issue—had elapsed.

The unprecedentedly large net purchases of Defence Bonds in 1958-59 to 1960-61 must obviously be associated with the fact that the yield on the new issue made in May, 1958 was for the first time fixed on a level with, if not slightly above, the prevailing long-term interest rate: the investor was in fact getting 5 per cent on six-month

[1]On the contrary on 1st May, 1960 the maximum purchase of the Tenth Issue was increased from £750 to £900.
[2]Increased from £2,000 in June, 1960.

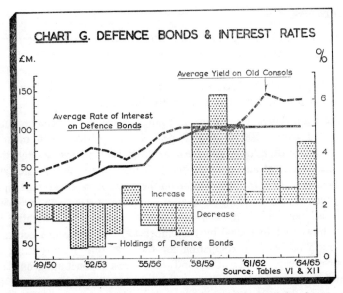

money. Moreover it might well have appeared that the long-term
rate was more likely to fall somewhat than to rise over the minimum
life of the Bonds. A similar expectation might have been entertained
for the earlier part of 1954-55, the only previous year when holdings
of Defence Bonds experienced a net increase: the long-term rate was
then falling rapidly towards the yield on Defence Bonds, and indeed
at one point the yield on Old Consols touched it. A further factor
assisting the performance of Defence Bonds in 1958-59 to 1960-61
may have been that prospective purchasers were then reaching their
maximum holdings of even more attractive National Savings media,
viz., National Savings Certificates (p. 87) and Premium Bonds.

After 1960, net purchases of Defence Bonds fell to low levels, until
their sale was superseded in May 1964 by that of National Development Bonds, which produced a net gain in 1964-65, taking the new
and old Bonds together, of about £92 million. The new Bonds, also
carrying interest at 5 per cent, mature in five years with a tax-free
bonus of £2 per £100 and are encashable at *one* month's notice. They
are thus a still more liquid form of investment.

Thus the experience of Defence and National Development Bonds
reinforces the evidence of the sensitivity of potential investors in
National Savings both to interest rates and to liquidity.

4. Premium Bonds

From their inception in November 1956 to March 1960—three years and a half—net sales of Premium Bonds, as 'Premium Savings Bonds' are commonly called, amounted to about £250 million.   Since then their popularity has been well sustained, with an average annual net intake of over £45 million, not greatly fluctuating.

Premium Bonds, the maximum holding of which has been gradually increased from £500 to £1,000 per person, participate in monthly prize draws after they have been held six full months, though they are encashable at any time on demand. The prize fund is calculated at the rate of 4 per cent per annum on the value of the bonds participating; but the chance of a prize (varying in amount from £25 to £1,500) had declined from 1 in 9,600, at which it stood immediately after the first draw, to 1 in 10,900 by November 1959.[1] The decline occurs as the ratio of bonds participating for the first time (contributing six months' interest to the prize fund) to the rest (contributing only one month's interest) falls.   Thus, with a growing fund the value of the chance tends to decline towards a theoretical 4 per cent from the initial level of about 5.2 per cent.

Prizes are not liable to tax, so that the average gross interest to be expected was initially about 9 per cent for the standard rate income-tax payer (and correspondingly more for the surtax payer) in 1957 and is still well above 7 per cent.[2] It is not therefore surprising either that such relatively large sums were invested in Premium Bonds over the first two or three years of the scheme or that, according to figures given in July 1957[3], well over half the Bonds purchased in the first two months of the scheme were in denominations of £100 to £500, or that the annual net investment in the Bonds has progressively declined. Apart from any spice of a gamble, the attraction of investing the maximum amount in Premium Bonds for the taxpayer (or his wife) who is liable at the standard or higher rates has been very strong. On the other hand, despite the ease of encashment, the advantages can usually only be reaped at the expense of liquidity, by leaving the Bonds untouched for considerable periods—whence the low but rising ratio of encashment to investment (£38 million against about £290

---

[1]Hansard, 19th November, 1959, coln. 1337.
[2]Taking account of the reduced rate of tax since April 1959.
[3]Hansard, 23rd July, 1957, Written Answers, coln. 42.

million in the first three-and-a-half years), but £192 million against £683 million in the whole eight-and-a-half years.

5. *Conclusion*

A study of the individual forms of National Savings over the last decade and a half confirms the initial impression that National Savings have now remarkably little connection with saving. The idea that National Savings represent the meritorious activities of the thrifty poor amassing 'small savings' by a steady process of self-denial may once upon a time have had reality. If so, it was already losing it between the wars, when a study[1] produced evidence that, in contrast with the period before 1914,

> "the non-wage earning classes have contributed considerable sums to savings deposits, the rate of increase of which has tended to vary inversely with the rates of increase in the amounts of Government stock held (by the savings banks for depositors) and of National Savings Certificates".

Likewise the Colwyn Committee on National Debt and Taxation, while quoting the Montagu Committee of 1922 to the effect that "at least half" the total (of National Savings Certificates) sold up to 31st March, 1922 "represented subscriptions by those classes whose needs the Certificates were primarily intended to meet", reported in 1927 (Cmd 2800, para. 57) that "it is certain that a very large volume is held outside the working classes".

By now, the notion has lost all contact with reality. It is impossible to reconcile the sensitivity of the various forms of National Savings to interest rates prevailing generally and to considerations of liquidity with any idea that their movements represent a rise or fall in the propensity of the 'small saver' to save. The natural explanation of the phenomena is that overwhelmingly they represent switching from one form of investment to another and that these switches are the activity for the most part of investors liable to tax at standard or higher rates. Indeed, where tax-free interest or the equivalent is obtainable, the significant influence of the surtax payer, though it cannot be proved, may reasonably be suspected.

Taking the last sixteen years' experience, the result of the first

[1]Radice, l.c., p. 55.

nine, put together, was a substantial net outflow of cash from the Government; but even in the last seven, when there was an average net inflow of about £200 million a year, it cannot be concluded that the Government and the National Savings Movement had succeeded in 'mobilising small savings' or 'stimulating additional saving'. What they had done was to attract to the Government in the form of National Savings, largely through the realisation of other assets, money which would in any case have been lent (directly or indirectly) either to the Government or to other borrowers.

The important question about National Savings in the second half of the twentieth century is whether it is a good thing for the Government to borrow *in this form* what it intends to borrow anyhow. Whatever the penalties attached to encashment of the different kinds of National Savings, they are in fact all virtually 'at call'. The question is therefore whether the Government ought to increase these 'sight' liabilities by borrowing further on National Savings terms.

The net rates offered on most forms of National Savings, plotted on Chart H, have straddled the yields on short-dated (four to five year) Government securities and kept below the yields on long-dated. But there are two important additional factors. In the first place, the Government has to a large extent been paying these rates of interest tax-free; and secondly, the cost of selling and administering National Savings is exceptionally high. For instance, on 2½ per cent savings bank deposits the National Debt Commissioners were paying the banks £2 17s. 6d. per cent up to 1957 and £3 2s. 6d. since; the National Savings Committee receives an annual vote of about £1½ million.

Thus, up to 1957-58, in order to avoid meeting in cash any appreciable part of about £6,000 million 'sight' liabilities in the form of National Savings, the Government was having to offer higher rates of interest than it needed to pay on other comparably short borrowing, to incur higher management expenditure and to offer substantial tax advantages. Even so it barely succeeded: the Post Office Savings Bank and Defence Bonds were each responsible for heavy net outflows of cash. This is what the Treasury meant when they told the Radcliffe Committee (para. 101): "we have to work very hard to stand still in this".

Then in 1958-59 and since the Government succeeded, by the inducements explained above, in borrowing an average of about

£200 million each year in the form of National Savings rather than in the form of dated securities. On the other hand, the Government's 'sight' liabilities were increased by an appreciable percentage

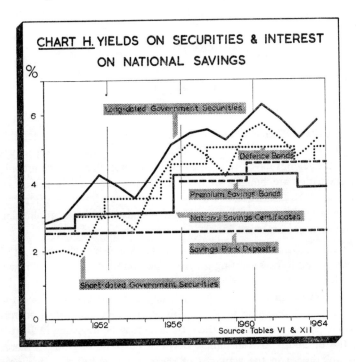

each year. What is more important, in a period when the Government was virtually unable to borrow in any other form, reliance upon National Savings probably contributed to deter those changes of policy which were necessary if the Government's credit with the public was to be restored.

It is permissible to doubt whether the balance of advantage does not lie against a further increase in National Savings and whether the long-term aim should not be, over the years, to convert more and more National Savings into other and less liquid forms of Government debt. The evidence of recent years suggests that the costly and not entirely risk-free effort to increase the total of National Savings could be reversed without diminishing such opportunities as they afford for genuine 'small saving' in the traditional sense.

CHAPTER VII

SECURITIES

The purchase of securities out of income represents one of two possible transactions. If the securities are bought from the body which issues them, the savings have been placed at its disposal. Far more commonly the securities are bought second-hand, from some other person or body. In this case there is merely an exchange of assets—often one link in a whole chain of such exchanges—and the ultimate application of the savings is unascertainable.

Common parlance is here misleading. A person who buys steel shares is said to be 'investing in steel'. Yet unless the shares are newly issued by the steel company, he is doing no such thing, except in the unlikely event that the vendor (or some successor of his along the line) uses the purchase money in his turn to buy new steel shares. Otherwise, for all he knows, the purchaser may be investing in British plastics or South African mines. Between purchase of paid-up shares and investment in the activities of the relevant industry or business there is at most this connection: an increase in the demand for a particular kind of security tends to raise its price, and conversely to lower the yield obtainable by purchasing it; consequently undertakings of the kind in question can obtain money for investment at a lower cost than before, and may to that extent be encouraged or enabled to increase their investment.

The ascertainable effects of the purchase of securities are thus to be measured by the total value of newly-created securities which are sold to the public in a given period. The volume of Government (or Government-guaranteed) stocks and of various types of other securities which have been issued and sold over the last seventeen years is shown in Tables XIV and XV. The latter data are necessarily

96

defective because they stop short at the securities of public companies: no similar figures are available for the creation and sale of shares in private companies.

Table XIV shows the Government's net receipts from the public by sale of Government and Government-guaranteed securities (other than Treasury Bills and National Savings) in the fourteen financial years 1951-52 to 1964-65.

Table XV shows the value for which new issues of securities, other than Government and Government-guaranteed securities, have been sold to the public annually since 1948.

The contrast presented by the two Tables is striking. From a high level in 1951-52—the statistics, prepared originally for the Radcliffe Committee, go no further back—net borrowing by the Government through sale of securities to the public fell after 1956 to less than nothing. In the six years 1951-52 to 1956-57 the Government raised £2,156 million, or over £350 million a year on average, by the sale of its securities. In the eight subsequent years, from 1957-58 to 1964-65, it actually had to find over £100 million from other sources to meet encashments of maturities. True, there was an occasional 'good' year, such as 1962-63, when the prospect of interest rates falling rendered it attractive for a short time to buy gilt-edged securities. But taking one year with another, the fact is that the Government has long ceased to be able to borrow from the public at all in the normal manner. In the same period of fourteen years, the annual volume of non-Government new issues sold to the public has more than doubled, and that of new issues by public companies has more than trebled. In this dramatic reversal of roles, there were three points of specially sharp change: 1954, when Government sales fell almost to nothing while issues by public companies practically doubled; 1957, when Government sales turned sharply negative; and 1959, when company issues nearly doubled again.

Purchases of new securities are financed, directly or indirectly, not only from personal but from corporate savings and from cash or bank deposits; and a comparison with the total of personal savings (Table IV) shows no significant correlation. On the other hand there is a very marked correlation (Chart I) between company issues and the prices of ordinary shares.

Some caution is necessary in interpreting the meaning of this correlation. Unlike most of the channels of saving discussed so far, the

TABLE XIV
GOVERNMENT SECURITIES SOLD TO THE PUBLIC

				£m.[1]	£m.[2]
1951-52	..	..	..	834	—
1952-53	..	..	..	433	—
1953-54	..	..	..	459	—
1954-55	..	..	..	18	—
1955-56	..	..	..	232	—
1856-57	..	..	..	180	—
1957-58	..	..	..	−110	—
1958-59	..	..	..	−64	−71
1959-60	..	..	..	−512	−519
1960-61	..	..	..	—	292
1961-62	..	..	..	—	−32
1962-63	..	..	..	—	298
1963-64	..	..	..	—	33
1964-65	..	..	..	—	−6

Sources: [1]Annual Abstract of Statistics, 1964.
[2]New series, Bank of England Quarterly Bulletin, Vol. I, no. 5, Vol. V, no. 2.

volume of new issues of securities is not determined solely by the saver. Whereas, for instance, the Government stands ready to accept National Savings in whatever quantity they are forthcoming, and the building societies place no practical restriction upon deposits or shares, the investor cannot buy more new securities than companies and other borrowers decide to issue. In fact, the movement of new issues is a resultant of the combined decisions of borrowers and lenders; and the borrowers may be influenced by such matters as the state and prospects of trade, which are not related at all directly or simply to share prices. Nevertheless, the correlation does strongly suggest that a rise in the value of existing shares has encouraged the issue and the absorption of new shares, and that a fall in their value has had the opposite effect.

From the borrowers' point of view, a period of high share prices is one which offers the advantage of borrowing at a low rate of interest. From the lenders' point of view the prospect of an increase in the capital value of their investment has outweighed any disincentive effect of falling yields. It may also be that when short-term interest rates are high, a high yield combined with liquidity outweighs in attraction a high yield combined with illiquidity but with a prospect of capital appreciation, and that this explains the similarity between the behaviour of new company issues and of certain forms of National Savings in 1958 (pp. 89-90, 94).

TABLE XV

NON-GOVERNMENT NEW ISSUES: 1948 to 1964

Year	Home Companies	Of which banking, finance, etc.[1]	Local authorities	Public Boards	Of which nationalised industries[2]	Overseas bodies	Total
	1	2	3	4	5	6	7
1948	113·8	5·0	—	99·5	99·5	38·1	251·4
1949	95·5	9·1	—	—	—	43·0	138·5
1950	107·9	5·8	—	154·4	148·5	50·7	313·0
1951	127·9	8·0	—	75·5	73·5	48·7	252·1
1952	117·2	7·6	—	205·8	205·8	47·4	307·4
1953	91·8	13·1	19·4	226·1	204·0	58·7	396·0
1954	185·5	42·3	18·2	206·3	181·0	61·1	471·1
1955	219·4	37·5	8·8	296·9	296·0	42·1	567·2
1956	210·7	41·1	53·9	—	—	31·3	295·9
1957	293·8	33·9	24·2	2·9	—	62·4	383·3
1958	179·5	30·7	60·9	14·7	—	61·4	316·5
1959	385·0	146·8	45·2	5·0	—	45·2	480·4
1960	457·1	118·9	52·5	4·8	—	42·3	556·7
1961	524·3	162·5	29·2	—	—	55·2	608·7
1962	386·0	131·6	155·4	23·8	—	39·8	605·0
1963	431·2	110·5	94·5	8·9	—	58·4	593·0
1964	384·7	75·4	79·9	—	—	43·4	508·0
1965	500·0	40·1	264·1	—	—	6·4	770·5

Source: Midland Bank

1 Including some overseas issues shown under col 6.

2 Since 1955 nationalised industries are financed through the Exchequer.

<u>CHART I</u>. ISSUES, YIELDS & PRICES

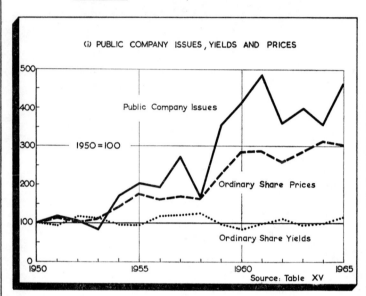

(i) PUBLIC COMPANY ISSUES, YIELDS AND PRICES

Public Company Issues

1950 = 100

Ordinary Share Prices

Ordinary Share Yields

Source: Table XV

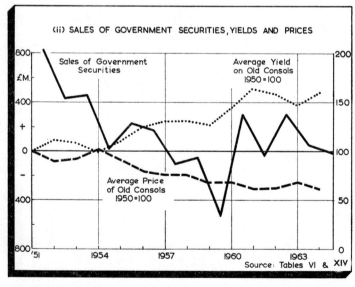

(ii) SALES OF GOVERNMENT SECURITIES, YIELDS AND PRICES

Sales of Government Securities

£M.

Average Yield on Old Consols 1950 = 100

Average Price of Old Consols 1950 = 100

Source: Tables VI & XIV

The correlation also suggests that the controls exercised during the 1950s over the issue of new securities—not merely the unofficial 'marshalling of the queue of borrowers' by the Bank of England but also the overt restraint applied by the Capital Issues Committee—did not influence the trend appreciably. During one period of intensified control in 1951-53 new issues fell somewhat; during another, 1955-57, they continued to rise. The behaviour of the graph agrees with the Radcliffe Committee's "impression . . . that the effect of the capital issues control as it has been operated in the 1950s . . . upon the pressure in the new issue market was very slight indeed" (para. 463).

In contrast with the sales of non-Government new issues, the sales to the public of Government and Government-guaranteed fixed-interest securities appear to show the effect of two influences. First, there is the general and dramatic downward trend from the still high levels of the early 1950s to the low levels and net outflow of the late 1950s and early 1960s. There can be little doubt that this trend represented the deepening sense that inflation was likely to be a permanent state of affairs and the consequent disinclination to acquire

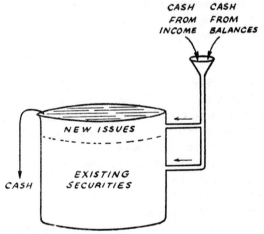

fixed-interest securities[1]. Within this long-term trend, however, there may be a certain short-term responsiveness to yields. Hence the inverse relationship between the price of Old Consols[2] and the sales of Govern-

[1] In the ten years 1956 to 1965 £100 invested at 2½% earned a real rate of interest of approximately *minus* ¾%.

[2] There is no material difference if the price of long-dated Government securities is taken instead (cf. p. 52).

ment or Government-guaranteed securities which produces a certain 'scissors effect' in the sales and price lines on Chart I (ii).

Thus the combined picture of new securities as a whole reflects the predominant influence of concern to preserve or increase the real value of investments, especially against a background of more or less continuous inflation; but the influence of the rate of interest is still very much alive as a secondary factor.

The diagram above illustrates what happens in the purchase and sale of securities. The amount of money (whether income, i.e. savings, or not) which is spent in any given period on purchasing securities is always equal to the amount of money realised by the sale of existing securities *plus* the value of new securities issued and sold during the period.

The net investment in securities cannot exceed the value of the new issues: any increase in the amount of money offered for securities without a corresponding increase in the total of securities merely means an equivalent increase in the outflow of money into other channels.

It follows that if net purchases of securities by one class of investor equal the amount of new securities created and sold, the purchases and sales of securities by all other classes of investor put together must have cancelled out; and this proposition holds good both of securities as a whole and also of any particular type of security, such as Government stocks or ordinary shares. For example, we know (p. 75) that net purchases of the equity of United Kingdom public companies by life assurance and superannuation funds in 1957 and 1963 appreciably exceeded the value of new equity of the same type created in that year. It therefore follows that there was not only no net increase in such holdings by other investors taken as a whole, but an actual decrease.

Moreover, if those other investors include, as they do, classes whose holdings of such securities are known to have also increased, then those of the remaining classes of investor must have diminished correspondingly. The growth of investment and unit trusts is significant in this connection. Take the example of 1963, when purchases of U.K. public company shares by life assurance and superannuation funds exceeded sales of new shares by about £160 million. In the same year, £110 million was used by investment and unit trusts in the purchase of U.K. public company shares. It follows that there must have been a decline of some £270 million in similar holdings in other hands.

It seems certain that the same is true of Government securities, of which life and superannuation funds and unit trusts continued to increase their holdings in years such as 1957 when there has been no net sale by the Government to the public (see Tables X and XIV).

The remaining classes of investor, who have accommodated these net increases by liquidating their holdings and applying the proceeds elsewhere, have been the personal sector, corporations and (in the case of gilt-edged securities) the banks. There are no figures for, nor means of deducing, the holdings of securities by corporations; but some indication of the holdings of the personal sector can be gained from the analysis of estates becoming liable to estate duty year by year. Table XVI shows the securities comprised in estates on which duty was paid over the last decade or so, and adjusts the values in accordance with the appropriate indices of security prices.

TABLE XVI

SECURITIES IN ESTATES PAYING DEATH DUTIES:
1948/49 to 1963/64

£ million

Year	British Government & Government-guaranteed securities			Shares, etc., in British public companies		
	Valuation	Price index [1]	At 1950 prices	Valuation	Price index [2]	At 1950 prices
	1	2	3	4	5	6
1948-49	144·6	102·5	141·1	n.a.	105·7	—
1949-50	155·4	102	152·4	n.a.	98·4	—
1950-51	151·8	100	151·8	n.a.	100	—
1951-52	155·6	96·9	160·6	n.a.	116·3	—
1952-53	132·5	87·4	151·6	149·6	101·2	147·8
1953-54	143·3	92·1	155·6	149·9	110·5	135·7
1954-55	163·3	98·3	166·1	186·1	141·3	131·7
1955-56	136·3	89·1	153	178·7	175·5	101·8
1956-57	129·6	79·4	163·2	175·2	162·6	107·8
1957-58	118·1	76·9	153·6	174·4	169·5	102·9
1958-59	121·8	77·1	158·0	194·3	163·7	118·7
1959-60	128·3	83·2	154·2	256·9	225·2	114·1
1960-61	118·6	77·9	152·2	281·7	286·8	98·2
1961-62	126·6	73·7	171·8	315·1	287·8	109·5
1962-63	130·8	78·2	167·3	325·7	257·0	126·7
1963-64	127·5	85·1	149·8	374·1	285·2	131·2

Source: *Annual Reports of the Commissioners of Inland Revenue*, H.M.S.O.
    [1]The long-dated securities index for the nearest corresponding calendar year (*Annual Abstract of Statistics*).
    [2]The ordinary shares index, *ibid.*, (*Financial Times* Index of ordinary shares (1 July, 1935 = 100) recalculated on base average 1950 = 100).

The reliability of the result is subject to severe qualification. For example, estates valued under £5,000 (£3,000 before 1962, £4,000 before 1963, £2,000 before 1954) do not feature at all; the composition of estates paying death duties in a particular year may not accurately reflect that of personal estates at the time taken as a whole; the indices of security prices can at best be only roughly appropriate, because the different classes of security (debenture, preference, ordinary, etc.) are not distinguished in the Inland Revenue statistics. Moreover, there are shifts between categories from one year to another: shares in private companies become shares in public companies by a change in the status of the companies, and shares in private and public companies are being created all the time by incorporation. These are mere alterations in the classification of assets, unrelated to the movement of assets between different classes of holders, with which we are concerned in studying securities as a channel of savings. Finally, there is a certain fluctuation from year to year in the total number of estates on which death duties are paid.

Nevertheless, Table XVI strongly suggests that personal holdings of Government and Government-guaranteed securities have remained relatively stable while personal holdings of public company equity have fallen fairly steadily until the last two years,[1] and thus tends to support the conclusion reached above by considering the relationship between new issues and net purchases.

If we now look at the net increase in assets in the form of securities, which, as already demonstrated, is equivalent to the value of new issues sold to the public, there are only two sources from which this increase can be financed: net savings (i.e. out of income) or net reduction of cash balances. In practice, as we have seen, the net increase is amply accounted for in recent years by net saving through life assurance and superannuation funds alone. There is therefore no net reduction of cash balances through the purchase of securities. Cash balances and savings which are applied directly or indirectly to the purchase of securities over and above the amount of the net increase in securities are simply being shunted from one hand to another through the market in securities.

The proportion of the money thus shunted which represents personal savings is probably considerable; but there is no means of

[1] Recent figures are subject to substantial revision.

quantifying it. For example, the smallness of the average holding in unit trusts and the comparatively small amounts in which units are usually purchased suggest, though they do not prove, that there is a considerable element of personal savings (as opposed to transfers of existing assets) in the funds which the trusts apply to the purchase of securities. An investigation[1] based on 1,600 replies from clients of stockbrokers and unit trusts who have £1,000 or less invested or whose weekly income does not exceed £50 showed that the sources of finance for purchases of shares or units were, in order of importance, current income and bank account, and then (half as frequently) National Savings.

If more personal savings are applied, directly or through trusts, to the purchase of the securities of public companies, then, assuming no reduction in the volume of the company savings and the cash balances which are also so applied, two results must follow: there will be an increase in the amount of personal savings shunted through the securities market and flowing out again into other channels, and the price level of securities will rise unless kept down by an increase in the quantity of securities, i.e. by an increase in new issues and in conversions of private companies and unincorporated businesses into public companies. Let us assume for simplicity that the latter cause of increase—public incorporation—is not a variable which depends on the price level of public company securities. We may then say that, other things being equal, an increase in the amount of personal savings applied to the purchase of the securities of public companies will tend to stimulate new issues. Upon this result depends any economic case that can be made for 'encouraging' or 'facilitating' investment of personal savings in equities.

Every market costs something to maintain: it is the price which has to be paid for the service which the market performs. The preceding argument has treated as net the input and outflow of money through the market in securities and has ignored, as an item of current consumption, the costs of buying and selling them.

The costs of the securities market, other than fiscal, are in inverse ratio to the size of the sums applied to the purchase of securities. The relative cost of brokerage is dauntingly high on small purchases;

[1] *Wider Shareholding*, Acton Society Trust, 1959. A recent Stock Exchange enquiry (*The Times*, 13 May, 1966) showed that 93 per cent of adults in Britain have savings, in the following order of frequency: (1) life assurance (63 per cent), (2) Premium Bonds, (3) Post Office, trustee and commercial banks, (4) National Savings Certificates, (5) building societies, (6) stocks and shares (7 per cent).

even so, it has been estimated[1] that the charges on transactions of under £300 do not cover the stockbroker's total expenses, and those on transactions of under £75 do not cover his direct expenses. With small isolated investments it is also impossible to reduce risk by securing an adequate spread over different securities and types of security, or by employing expert investment advice and management.

These deterrents to the investment of small sums in securities are counteracted by the institution of the unit trusts, which for a fixed initial and running charge cover the costs of buying and selling securities, provide expert investment and management, and spread the total sum subscribed over a wide range of high-class securities. The purchaser of units is at no advantage or disadvantage according to the size of his total investment or individual purchases, and has the benefit of perfect marketability, since the managers stand ready at all times to repurchase units at a price corresponding to the current value of the underlying securities less a small, known discount.

On the other hand, while the unit trust method thus eliminates a great part of the risk of investment in securities and the obstacles to small investment, it also, of necessity, largely eliminates the social and political advantages which are sometimes claimed for "the closer association of wage earners and other small savers with the financing of industry".[2] The investor is not brought into touch as a shareholder with the fortunes or management of firms; he has no concern with or knowledge of the problems and prospects of the businesses or industries whose securities underlie the units; and he has no responsibility or voice (beyond the selection of his trust) in the direction of the purchase of securities.

The market in securities, in addition to its operating costs, is also subject to a turn-over tax. The total of stamp duties paid on 'stocks, shares, debentures, etc.' in recent years is shown in Table XVII. It would not be correct to relate these sums directly with the amounts of money raised by the sale of new securities by the Government, by other public authorities and by public companies, and to say, for example, that in the thirteen years 1951-52 to 1963-64 about £450 million was paid in duty while about £7,000 million was raised in this way (Tables

[1] P. Montague, *Stock Exchange Gazette*, February 1959, quoted in *Wider Shareholding* (*supra cit.*, p. 13), which also has a valuable comparison (p. 18) between American and British market costs.
[2] *Everyman a capitalist: some proposals for the small saver in industry*, Conservative Political Centre, 1959.

TABLE XVII

YIELD OF STAMP DUTY ON TRANSFER OF SECURITIES:

1948/49 to 1963/64

	£ million			£ million
1948-49	... 19·7	**1956-57**	...	24·9
1949-50	... 15·0	**1957-58**	...	25·1
1950-51	... 18·1	**1958-59**	...	33·0
1951-52	... 20·7	**1959-60**	...	59·5
1952-53	... 15·1	**1960-61**	...	48·8
1953-54	... 22·1	**1961-62**	...	51·3
1954-55	... 34·7	**1962-63**	...	49·3
1955-56	... 26·7	**1963-64**	...	40·0

Source: *Annual Reports of the Commissioners of Inland Revenue.*

XIV and XV)—a ratio of over 6 per cent. Not only do the figures for duty relate to all other types of security as well (e.g. shares in private companies) but the functions of a market include the exchange of existing assets no less than the disposal of new ones.

Nevertheless, it can be argued that a tax upon the transactions in a market increases its imperfection and thus renders it less efficient in performing its economic function. For a tax has a distorting effect if it applies to one market and not to another, or more severely to one market than to another. These objections apply to stamp duty on transactions in securities, inasmuch as it is not payable on National Savings or building society shares, and is either not payable at all or payable only at lower rates on transactions in real estate, while a number of applications of savings—bank deposits, for example—are outside the scope of stamp duty altogether. It may therefore be claimed that stamp duty must exert *some* diversionary effect, however small, upon the direction of the flow of savings.

Another fiscal influence is the fact that income tax at the standard rate is deducted at source from the payment of interest upon nearly all securities, and that consequently security-holders who are liable at a lower rate, or not at all, have to reclaim the tax overpaid. Such persons are thereby under some inducement to prefer alternative applications of savings, where other things are equal or finely balanced. Here again it is impossible to gauge the practical effect. Certainly if the number of non-standard rate income-tax payers who earn dividends or interest, e.g. through unit trusts, were to increase greatly, over-payment of tax and consequential recovery would become a trouble-some problem; and already some hire purchase finance companies consider it worth while, in order to attract deposits from persons with low incomes, to offer interest on a quarterly rather than an annual basis and thus be able to pay it gross. However, it is hard to see any practicable remedy short of altering an established principle in tax collection which undoubtedly works in general to the benefit of the revenue and thus of the taxpayer at large. The proposal to exempt small amounts of investment income from tax altogether is discussed later (p. 131); but that is an essentially different matter.

At the beginning of this section the assumption was made that the purchase of securities from the body which issues them places the equivalent purchasing power at the disposal of that body. This assumption requires substantial qualification. If a steel company sells new shares to the public, it may, and usually does, apply part of the proceeds to the creation of new fixed capital for the production of steel. To this extent it is correct to say that the purchase money has been 'invested in steel', though, if the outlay does not take place in the same period as the issue, there will in the meantime have been some kind of switching operation by which the cash was temporarily exchanged for other assets, such as short-term debt.

However, the cash realised by the sale of the new issue may be, and often is, used to pay off existing debts of the company, particularly bank overdrafts. There is apparently no recent information on the extent to which new issues are thus applied; but an investigation[1] which covered a high proportion of the new issues in 1932 and 1933 showed that in those years, taken together, while 42.5 per cent of the proceeds was applied to new material capital, 35.5 per cent was used to repay debt, and the remaining 22 per cent for other purposes, such as the purchase of existing securities. It follows that where, as in recent years, the new issues (i.e. the net increases in securities) are financed by personal savings, only a part

[1] Radice, l.c., p. 96.

of those savings—perhaps less than half—may be directly invested in the undertakings concerned. The rest is, once again, shunted. If the proceeds of the sale of the new shares are used to purchase existing securities, there is merely 'double counting' and the effect is the same as the sale of trust units or investment company shares to the same value. If the proceeds are used repay bank advances, and the banks retain their advances at the same level, the result is to invest the equivalent of the savings in the undertakings financed by the new advances.

CHAPTER VIII

CASH AND BANK DEPOSITS

The most immediate form in which income is retained unspent by the recipient is the form in which he receives it. This is almost always either notes and coin or else 'bank money', that is, credit with one of the clearing banks, conveyed to him by a cheque or banker's order, or by some other document which is convertible into such credit. The recipient may keep the notes and coin in his possession. He may add the credit to his existing credit with a clearing bank, and do no more about it.

Though apparently different only in form, these two methods of saving also differ profoundly in their economic effects.

There is no objective definition of the point on the line between keeping sixpence in the pocket from one day to the next and sewing currency notes (or, when they were cash, gold sovereigns) into a mattress, at which the operation becomes hoarding. It is perhaps best to say that hoarding begins where coin or notes are retained longer or in larger amounts than serves the convenience of the saver. A person may renounce the advantages of security, interest or profit to be had by saving in other forms either because he distrusts, disbelieves or even is unaware of those advantages, or he may have adventitious reasons for preferring coin and notes—to steer clear, perhaps, of the police or the Inland Revenue.

The economic significance of hoarding lies not in the reduction of the supply of currency, but in the reduction of demand. As there is no "statutory or other restraint on the supply of cash",[1] the withdrawal from circulation by hoarding of even considerable quantities of coin and notes would have in itself no appreciable practical effect.

[1]*Radcliffe Report*, para. 376.

The practical effect of saving which takes the form of hoarding is that the claim on goods and services which the income saved represents is not, as in other forms of saving, transferred or exerted, but actually suppressed.

An increase in hoarding, therefore, unless its effects are otherwise counterbalanced, must produce a fall in the demand for, and therefore in the production of, goods and services. The effect is the same where the hoarding takes the form of an unused bank deposit. Income is received either as currency or as 'bank money'. Whether it is received as currency and deposited with a clearing bank or whether it is received in the first place as 'bank money', for example, by cheque, the saver leaves deposited with the bank the portion of it which he saves. That is, he neither converts it into cash nor draws cheques upon it. In this case the saving becomes what is called an 'idle balance'— 'bank money' which is inert, just as cash is inert when sewn into a sock; and the economic consequences are the same.

It is worth emphasising that these ill effects are not produced by retaining savings in any other form except currency. They do not follow, for example, from saving by the accumulation of precious metals and stones or of *objets* (whether *d'art* or otherwise). In any such case the claim on goods and services represented by the savings is in fact either exerted or transferred. If a man hoards new Staffordshire figurines, he exerts that much demand for the output of Staffordshire producers of pottery. If he hoards old china, he transfers his claim on resources to those who have old china to sell, and incidentally he probably exerts a demand for the services of dealers in old china.

Unfortunately we are in no position to form an idea of the variation in personal holdings of currency, still less of the manner in which such variations might reflect saving in the form of hoarding. The statistics on the ownership of notes, coin, and 'bank money' are so unsatisfactory that a recent survey[1] found no means of accounting for the ownership of nearly half the estimated supply of cash (in that sense). It is impossible to say how far this gap relates to currency and how far to 'bank money'. As currency represents less than one-fifth of the estimated supply of cash held by the public (e.g. £1,552 million out of £8,984 million in 1955), it follows that neither hoarding

[1] E. Victor Morgan, 'Britain's cash—a statistical mystery', *The Banker*, March 1959.

nor loss, destruction nor export can account for more than a small part, if any, of the gap. Nevertheless it would be wrong to exclude the theoretical possibility of variations in hoarding. Moreover, there could be considerable fluctuations over comparatively short periods in the amount of income temporarily retained as currency: for example, an increase in wages, whether real or purely monetary, may be accompanied by an increase in the quantity of cash kept about the person or in the house.

What the trend of personal saving in this form may be is not easy to determine. Some guidance may be derived (cf. p. 103) from the analysis of personalty in estates becoming liable to death duties each year. The proportion of cash (almost exclusively 'cash at bank') rose steadily from 1947-48 until 1953-54. Thereafter it remained virtually constant until 1958-59, since when it has fallen again quite sharply. It does not seem that the elimination of estates between £2,000 and £3,000 after 1954, between £3,000 and £4,000 after 1962, and between

TABLE XVIII

CASH IN ESTATES PAYING DEATH DUTIES:
1947/48 to 1963/64

£ million

Year	Net capital value of personalty liable	Cash included in column 1	Column 2 as %age of column 1
	1	2	3
1947-48	672·1	74·7	11·1
1948-49	662·8	92·5	14·0
1949-50	668·5	102·2	15·3
1950-51	653·0	100·8	15·4
1951-52	676·9	111·6	16·5
1952-53	607·5	102·3	16·8
1953-54	605·6	113·4	18·7
1954-55	693·2	128·2	18·5
1955-56	618·9	113·7	18·4
1956-57	624·8	117·7	18·8
1957-58	624·3	116·5	18·7
1958-59	703·1	134·1	19·1
1959-60	773·0	136·8	17·7
1960-61	814·0	138·6	17·0
1961-62	889·4	149·3	16·8
1962-63	901·2	134·2	14·9
1963-64	940·9	132·5	14·1

Source: *Annual Reports of the Commissioners of Inland Revenue.*

£4,000 and £5,000 after 1963, can have had much to do with this result. On the other hand, the composition of estates becoming liable to duty is not necessarily a reliable guide to the movement of personal assets generally.

Again, the movement of personal net deposits with clearing banks (i.e. deposits of persons less advances to persons) is also not necessarily an indication of the trends of saving in the form of 'bank money'; for it may equally or preponderantly reflect exchange of assets with other sectors rather than changes in the direction of current personal saving. Nevertheless the fall in the ratio of such deposits[1] to net personal incomes in the last decade or more is impressive, and makes it appear unlikely that in recent years there has been much, if any, net saving in this form by the personal sector.

TABLE XIX

NET PERSONAL DEPOSITS AND INCOMES:

1944, 1951, 1954 and 1958

£ million

Year	Net personal deposits with the London clearing banks	Net personal incomes (Table IV, col. 4)	Column 1 as %age of column 2
	1	2	3
1944	1,423	7,569	18·8
1951	1,675	10,349	16·2
1954	1,862	12,617	14·8
1958	2,255	16,247	13·9

Source: *Radcliffe Report*, Table 22.

[1]The division of net deposits into 'deposit accounts' and 'current accounts' is little or no guide to 'idle balances'."From the point of view of economical policy, the total of balances on deposit account has to be reckoned as almost, but not quite, as relevant as are current account balances to the pressure of demand. Bankers, although they may sometimes speak of deposit accounts as more stable than current accounts, nevertheless in practice appear to lump all their deposit liabilities together, and to treat them as in effect repayable on demand" (*Radcliffe Report*, para. 131).

H

CHAPTER IX

BETTING AND GAMBLING

Betting and gambling are not usually thought of in connection with saving, but it would nevertheless be wrong to omit them from an account of the channels of personal saving.

From the point of view of the bettor, the amount which he stakes out of his income, less his winnings, may be regarded as consumption expenditure—expenditure on entertainment not unlike the price of a cinema ticket or a trip on the *Saucy Jane*. Viewing the bettors in the mass, we see their expenditure on entertainment to be similarly not the gross total staked, but that amount *less* the sums which return to them collectively as winnings. The difference represents the remuneration of the organisers, the cost of the man-power employed, and tax.

The winnings, on the other hand, represent a redistribution of income, and if in the relevant period they are not expended by the winners upon consumption, then that amount of income has been saved—theoretically by the bettors, practically by the winners. The distinction is well taken by Lydall,[1] referring to winnings in football pools:

> "The dividends paid out by the football pools are accumulations of capital out of the stakes contributed by football pool supporters, and in this sense they are the outcome of collective saving by this section of the population. Once the money has been staked, the act of saving has been performed: the football match results merely determine how the total fund shall be divided among the winners. The problem is: to whom is this act of saving to be attributed? It cannot be attributed to the winners because that would conflict with our concept that saving derives only from income. In principle, the problem could be solved by imputing a proportion of each person's stake as a contribution to saving; but this would be very laborious and would scarcely justify the collection of the necessary data."

The writer is however mistaken in saying that 'once the money has been staked, the act of saving has been performed.' If the winner

[1] See p. 51.

114

spends his winnings on iced lollies, then no saving, from the point of view of the individual or of the economy, has been done at all—any more than if the pool supporters had contributed the same sums instead to a charitable organisation which used them to provide turkey and plum pudding for the old folk at Christmas.

It is indeed upon the application of winnings in the hands of the winners that the whole relevance of betting to saving depends. The larger the sum won, the more likely it is that part, if not the whole, of it will not in the relevant period be laid out on consumption goods and services, that is, that it will be saved. Where very large winnings are concerned, as in the football pools, it is almost physically impracticable for them to be other than largely saved. No one, of course, can assert what would have been the fate of all those shillings and sixpences contributed by the bettors if they had not been collected together and deposited in large dollops in the laps of a few winners; but as these are sums which the bettors, in their individual view, have decided to devote to entertainment, it is unlikely that but for the existence of betting, gambling and the pools, they would have been applied to the purchase of Savings Certificates or unit trust units. As the *Royal Commission on Betting, Lotteries and Gambling 1948-51* (Cmd 8190) observed (para. 64):

"The significance of the part returned as winnings depends mainly on the manner in which that part of the amounts staked which is returned in the form of winnings is redistributed. This varies according to the type of gambling; if, as in football pool betting, a large proportion of the total amounts staked is distributed in the form of large prizes to a small number of individuals, the economic effects will be different from those which arise from a form of gambling, such as betting on horse-racing or dog-racing, in which the habitual bettor makes many bets and not infrequently wins small sums."

Unfortunately for saving, it seems certain that only a small proportion of the total winnings from betting, gambling, and lotteries are distributed in large sums—and of this small proportion the lion's share is probably attributable to the football pools. The Royal Commission assessed the stakes and winnings in the different forms of gambling, etc., in 1950 as shown in Table XX.

It is in accordance with this estimate that the 1954 Blue Book included £70 million for betting and gambling under the 'other services' heading of Consumers' Expenditure, and this figure with modifications has been carried forward in later years. The Royal Commission's figures are also the basis of Lydall's estimate (*op. cit.*, p. 110) of £30

TABLE XX

STAKES AND WINNINGS IN BETTING AND GAMBLING, 1950

£ million

Form of betting	Stakes	Deductions including tax	Winnings
1	2	3	4
Totalisator: horse racing	25·5	2·6	22·9
dogtracks	70	11·2	58·8
Bookmakers: On course: horses	50		
dogs	60	22·5	245
Off course	157·5 [1]		
Football pools	52	26	26
All other forms	n.a.	5	n.a.
Total	415 plus	67·3	347·7 plus

Source: *Royal Commission on Betting.*
[1] Average of highest and lowest estimates.

million as the amount of saving done through the football pools in 1951-52.

An enquiry into gaming instituted under the Finance Act, 1963, cast light on the 'other forms', about which the Royal Commission had no information, and disclosed expenditure of £10.3 million in a year on gaming machines, and of £14.4 million on other forms of gaming (mostly bingo).[1] In his Budget speech the next year[2] the Chancellor of the Exchequer estimated total annual expenditure on all forms of betting and gambling at between £100 million and £150 million, and total stakes at £400 million to £500 million.

If saving though this channel is in practice restricted to the field of large winnings, it would probably be wrong, in the light of the Royal Commission's estimates, to assess it at much more than one-tenth of total winnings (say, £50 million). This is not a large sum relatively to personal savings as a whole; on the other hand it would be wrong to overlook that, on balance and to something like this extent, betting and gambling and especially pools tend to increase rather than diminish the amount of personal income saved.

[1] Cmnd. 2275.
[2] *Hansard,* 14 April, 1964, coln. 246.

Part III

Conclusions

CHAPTER X

PERSONAL SAVING

The survey in Part II of the various forms in which personal income is saved and of their experience, so far as known, over the last sixteen or seventeen years is not the same thing as an analysis of the totals of personal saving deduced in Chapter IV by the 'residual' method. In the first place, one channel frequently overlaps another: part of the income saved, for example, by way of life assurance premia and superannuation contributions also features among the net purchases of securities; some of the income saved by way of repayments of mortgage or hire purchase debt is applied to making further loans or to other investment. Another difficulty is that too little is known of the growth in the volume of the various assets held by persons to permit of it being totalled up and equated with personal saving.

Nevertheless the survey points to some important conclusions about the factors which influence the direction, if not the total, of personal savings.

The factor which emerges as outstandingly powerful is the rate of interest, in particular the net rate of interest after payment of tax, if any. Its effect, however, is modified by two further factors: liquidity and prospect of appreciation. The behaviour of various forms of saving in years such as 1958, when short-term rates of interest were relatively high, suggests that liquidity—or encashability—exercises a certain attraction: if the sacrifice of interest is not serious, liquidity comes into play as a balancing consideration. On the other hand, a counter-attraction is exercised by the prospect of capital appreciation in money terms, or real terms, or both, which is equivalent to a rate of interest, reckoned to redemption, that is high both gross and net.

These conclusions are truisms in the sense that the operation of these factors would have been predicted *a priori* by the non-economist; but the promptitude and sensitivity with which the flow of savings into different channels has responded to them is impressive. It emphasises the importance of interest rates as a selector which determines the application of those resources that the private sector refrains from consuming. Here indeed it is seen that, as the Radcliffe Committee say—though speaking in this passage from the point of view of the borrower—"the rate of interest does influence the allocation of resources in favour of those projects which make the most of the real resources of the country" (para. 495). It follows that anything which causes relative rates of interest to reflect less perfectly or truthfully what 'makes the most of the real resources of the country' ought to be viewed askance.

Only the Government can in practice so operate on relative interest rates as to produce these effects on any large scale. It can, and does, give tax preference (and thus higher net rates of interest) to those who lend to it under certain conditions. It can, and sometimes does, reduce the rate at which it, and thus others, borrow from the public by 'open market operations', i.e. it forces up the price of its own existing securities by buying them with money procured through its unique power to tax or to borrow from the banking system. If the amount which the Government borrows from the public were limited to the amount it could raise at the rate of interest that it was prepared to pay, one might simply conclude that it ought to borrow, without tax preferences, at the market rate. In fact, the amount of expenditure which the Government finances by borrowing is not limited in this way: governments do not allow their expenditure to be 'choked off' by the interest rate. Therefore at whatever rates the government borrows, the distribution of resources between itself and other borrowers or potential borrowers remains arbitrary. Theoretically it would be correct to say that government expenditure financed by borrowing is incompatible *per se* with the idea of using the rate of interest 'to allocate resources in favour of those projects which make the most of the real resources of the country'. In practice the degree of this inevitable distortionary effect depends on the relative size of such expenditure.

In the recent years the Government in Britain has paid for its borrowing at well above the market rate in terms of net interest; for its net borrowing from the public has of late been almost wholly in the costliest forms of National Savings.[1] But the economic distortion would not be wholly removed if the Government were put on the same footing as regards interest rates as other borrowers, for example, by giving tax relief on the first £15 of *all* investment income, or by allowing the price of government securities to fall until the Government's needs could all be met in the market; for the distortion is partly implicit in the fact of the Government's net borrowing itself.

Another *a priori* assumption which the experience of the last decade and a half confirms is the stability of contractual savings and their tendency to increase at a steady rate. House mortgage repayments and life assurance and superannuation contributions are the chief magnitudes here, repayment of hire purchase debt being still relatively minor (p. 66). Chart J below shows that the trend of contractual savings (gross of house depreciation) is still not only growing steadily but also growing at a steadily increasing rate.

The fact that the *direction* in which personal savings flow is highly sensitive to the rate of interest does not by itself necessarily indicate that the *total* of personal savings is influenced by it. The decision to withhold a given amount of income from consumption might be taken if there were no prospect of interest at all or even if the true rate of

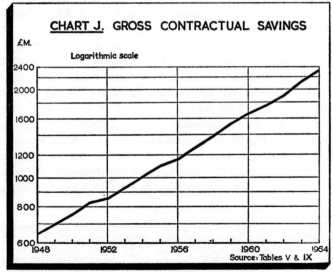

CHART J. GROSS CONTRACTUAL SAVINGS

£M.

Logarithmic scale

2400
2000
1600
1200
1000
800
600

1948   1952   1956   1960   1964

Source: Tables V & IX

[1] See Chapter VII.

interest were negative. Introspectively it is perfectly possible to distinguish the considerations which predispose an individual or a family to save from those which influence the disposal of those savings, once the decision to make them is taken.

On the other hand it would be highly paradoxical if savers were strongly influenced by reward in terms of interest in laying out their savings but not influenced by it *at all* in determining the amount of their income on which that reward was to be reaped. To take an extreme case, if people expected to double in a year whatever money they saved, would they not be likely to save more than if they expected their savings to earn no interest or, if you like, to be halved in value? If the answer is Yes—and surely it is—then there must be *some* positive relationship between rate of interest and flow of personal savings. The relationship may be slight; the elasticity of the total amount of savings in response to changes in rates of interest may be low; but still to some degree a positive relationship must exist.

The assumption of such a relationship is in practice unavoidable. It is curious that those who question both the elasticity of saving, and the inverse elasticity of investment, in relation to interest rates, nevertheless end by taking both for granted as a guide to action. Thus, the Radcliffe Committee "encountered extreme difficulty in testing the possibility that personal savings . . . are directly affected by changes in interest rates" (para. 450), and found that "when we confined our questions strictly to the direct effect of interest rate changes in making business men alter their decisions to buy or sell goods and services, we were met by general scepticism. The insignificance of interest charges . . . was emphasised to us again and again" (para. 451). Yet their recommendation (para. 496) is this: "If the authorities believe that *the pressure of demand for capital development is seriously out of gear with the available resources,* and is likely to remain so, it is essential that both by word and deed *they should promote a movement of long-term rates as well as short".* If this does not mean that the propensity to save and the desire to invest are elastic—not, of course, necessarily equally elastic—in relation to rates of interest, it means nothing.[1]

[1]This contradiction between practice and theory is beautifully enshrined in a single sentence elsewhere in the Radcliffe Committee's report (my italics): "We have found that stocks of commodities are extremely *insensitive to interest rates,* and in any case they are often financed with long-term capital, and could be much more widely so *if firms found this much cheaper"* (para. 489).

After all this it is difficult to ascribe merely to coincidence the correlation between estimated personal saving and long-term rates of interest, to which attention was drawn at the end of Chapter IV. That correlation is more than "the fact of increased saving in the 1950s".[1] The bare fact of an increase might indeed be explained satisfactorily by saying that, as the call on incomes to make good the wartime and post-war deficiencies "gradually exhausted itself, the proportion of unspent income naturally rose, without any great effort of abstention". A progressive change such as this, however, or such as the increase in personal real incomes, is inadequate to account for the phenomenon of saving and interest rates *moving up and down together*, a phenomenon which is rendered even more striking by the constancy with which the contractual component in total personal saving has been growing.

Certainly it may be assumed that an increase in net personal income is a condition which favours a general increase over a period in the proportion of that income saved, such as has been experienced in the last decade; for it would be inconceivable that a fall in net income diminishes the proportion saved—as at some point it must—but a rise does not at some point increase it.

It is in its effect on this figure of net income that the level of taxation of personal incomes has a relevance to saving. It may have it in two ways. First, of course, it determines the total net income (and thus the average net income per head) corresponding to a given total gross income. Secondly, however, it also determines the size of individual net incomes within that total, i.e. the order of variation about the mean. Since it is likely that, the larger an individual's net income, as well as a community's total net personal income, the greater will be the proportion of it that is saved, this second effect of taxation could also be significant: the more taxation tended to equalise net incomes, the less favourable to saving its effect would be, and *vice versa*. In practice it is difficult to detect any influence from this factor in the last decade and a half. Table XXI shows the proportion of the total income of all taxpayers after tax which was left to the 'top twentieth'.

Considering that this 'top slice' includes quite modest incomes—£800 net in 1938-39 or £1,500 net in 1960—it is clear that the distribution of net personal income has become less uneven not only since

[1] *Radcliffe Report,* para. 450.

TABLE XXI

NET INCOME OF LARGEST TAXPAYERS, 1938/39, 1949/50, 1954/55 and 1959/60 to 1962/63

Year	Total taxpayers '000	Net income of all taxpayers £m.	Income after tax £	Taxpayers '000	As % of total taxpayers (4 ÷ 1)	Net income received by taxpayers in Col. 4 £m.	Col. 6 as % of Col. 2.	Proportion of total net income received by 5% of taxpayers with the highest net incomes[1]
	1	2	3	4	5	6	7	8
1938-39	9,800	2,664	800+	397	4·1	610·6	22·9	28
1949-50	20,050	7,199	800+	1,265	6·3	1,384·5	19·0	15
1954-55	20,300	10,115	1,000+	1,295	6·4	1,713·0	16·9	13
1959-60	20,995	13,598	1,500+	973	4·6	1,878·0	13·8	15
1960-61	21,600	14,645	1,500+	1,124	5·2	2,136·0	14·6	14
1961-62	22,000	15,830	1,500+	1,395	6·3	2,686·0	17·0	13
1962-63	22,272	16,651	1,500+	1,565	7·0	3,066·7	18·4	13

Source: *Annual Reports of Commissioners of Inland Revenue.*

[1]These figures are approximations derived from columns 5 and 7.

before the war but probably since 1949-50, and certainly that the rise in personal saving has not coincided with any increase in concentration of net personal income.

In theory, saving should decline, other things being equal, in a community where the average age is rising, since it is both inherently likely, and to some extent borne out by observation,[1] that the proportion of income saved diminishes in the older age groups. The ageing in the last decade has been considerable, as Table XXII illustrates: the proportion of the adult population[2] which is aged 50 or more rose from 38.7 per cent to 44.2 per cent between 1951 and 1964. Other things, however, have not been equal. Not only the average expectation of survival to retirement but the average retirement age itself have been advancing: and these factors have been added to the others working for an increase in personal saving which have obliterated any retardatory effect of the changing age structure.

The period of increasing saving in the decade and a half has also been a period in which the value of money has fallen fairly rapidly, a period moreover which has been punctuated by phases of acute public consciousness of inflation and of fear that it had come to stay.

A United States Secretary of the Treasury is reported[3] as having said that "either the fear or the fact of inflation would in the long run lead to a shortage of savings to finance investment in plant and equipment that was essential to economic growth". Both *a priori* and also on the evidence, this appears to be the exact opposite of the truth. It is the channels through which income is saved, not the proportion of it which is saved, that are influenced by the saver's experience and expectations regarding the value of money. The natural consequence of actual or anticipated inflation is an increased preference for forms of saving where neither yield nor capital value is expressed in fixed monetary terms—that is, typically, the "plant and equipment . . . essential to economic growth". This is illustrated by the relative decline of saving in the form of building society shares (p. 62), National Savings (p. 81), and government securities (p. 98). In fact it is as likely that inflation—short, at least, of financial catastrophe—would increase, as that it would diminish, the total of personal income saved in all forms. The Royal Commission on Taxation were concealing

[1]Lydall, l.c., pp. 120 ff.
[2]Taken as those over 19.
[3]*The Times*, 22 February, 1960, p. 17.

TABLE XXII

AGE DISTRIBUTION OF POPULATION OVER 19: 1951, 1958 and 1964

Aged	1951		1958		1964	
	000's	%	000's	%	000's	%
1	**2**	**3**	**4**	**5**	**6**	**7**
20–29	21,879 } 13,846	61·2 } 38·7	20,973 } 15,341	57·8 } 42·3	20,825 } 16,468	55·8 } 44·2
50–64	8,377	23·4	9,357	25·8	10,036	26·9
65–	5,469	15·3	5,984	16·5	6,432	17·3
	35,725	100·0	36,314	100·0	37,293	100·0

Source: *Annual Abstract of Statistics*, 1959 and 1964; *Monthly Digest of Statistics*, March, 1965.

nonsense with a tone of high moral earnestness when they wrote (Cmd 9474, para. 59): "Any discussion of the topic of savings is a mere deployment of words unless it can take as its basis the assumption that a reasonable stability in the purchasing power of money is a fixed canon of public policy". Such stability has been anything but "a fixed canon of public policy"; but there is plenty to discuss about savings.

The effect of inflation on the channels (as opposed to the total) of saving can, of course, be partially or temporarily counteracted by the offer of higher monetary reward in terms of interest; but unless accompanied by a high degree of liquidity, so that the risk of capital loss is limited, the interest inducement must be very high indeed to be effective. The statement of the Radcliffe Committee (para. 572) that "in so far as people foresee a steady rise of prices of 2 per cent per annum, they will look for a 5 per cent rate of interest instead of 3 per cent" understates the differential because it assumes that the additional 2 per cent is tax-free, whereas in practice, of course, it is taxed (and progressively taxed) as income. Thus, a much higher rate of interest (dependent on the rate of tax assumed) would be necessary to compensate the purchaser of fixed interest securities redeemable after, say, 25 years for the effect of an annual inflation of 2 per cent. This has been reflected in recent experience: the government has been able to borrow only at a high net rate of interest combined with high liquidity (p. 95), and the yield on good-class equities, i.e. on investment in real assets, has fallen well below the current yield on fixed-interest securities.

Though inflation, or rather the anticipation of continued inflation, may not affect the total of personal saving, its unquestionable effect upon the channels of personal saving is an economic distortion. The decision of the saver in a climate of inflation reflects not only his choice between certain alternative forms of reward for saving or the spontaneous assessment of future demand, but also, and even preponderantly, a view upon the likely behaviour of the currency, which is not an economic judgment related to the beneficial use of resources but an essentially political judgment or guess about future variations in the standard of measurement. It is scarcely going too far to say, for example, that in recent years the saver has not enjoyed the traditional choice between retaining the capital value of his savings at a relatively low reward and accepting an element of capital risk in return for higher reward.

This distortion makes serious inroads into the efficiency of the 'market' for savings and, if carried beyond a certain point, could damage the case for the spontaneous, as opposed to the centrally directed, determination of the application of the community's saving. It is one of the grounds for asserting that the acceptance of a state of inflation is basically irreconcilable with the acceptance of a free economy.

CHAPTER XI

PUBLIC POLICY

The deductions for government policy and action in relation to saving that emerge from this study are limited in scope and negative in character. Policy is commonly considered in the context of *increasing* the proportion of personal income which is saved. This assumes that the proportion 'ought' to be higher than it is, and also, incidentally, that the Government knows either how much higher it ought to be or else that it ought to be so enormously higher that there is no practical purpose in discussing the precise 'right' level.

There is no justification for either of these assumptions. If there are potential workers unemployed, it is meaningful to say that there 'ought' to be demand for their labour; but it does not follow that this demand ought to be for one possible set of products of their labour rather than another, nor therefore that it ought to represent increased saving rather than increased consumption. If on the other hand all, or practically all, potential workers are employed, there is no objective standpoint from which it can be asserted that this adequate demand ought to result in higher proportion from saving and in lower proportion from consumption, or in other words that their effort should be redirected into employments which impose more 'waiting' on the community than in present circumstances is forthcoming. To say that individuals chronically underestimate future as compared with present advantage is merely an assertion, in different terms, of the same unprovable 'ought'.

It is true that a government which has decided to spend and lend more than its revenue—and this has been the almost invariable posture of British governments since 1945—must pray that personal (and also corporate) saving *in the form of lending to the Government* will be at least equal to the difference. In the eyes of such a government, saving *in this form* and up to this amount must appear 'a consummation devoutly to be wished'. But that is a different thing from a higher proportion of personal income saved altogether. If saving doubled and none of the addition to it was lent to the Government, the Government's predicament would be no whit improved, and this again has been substantially the experience of British governments in the last decade and a half.

If the Government must spend or lend above its revenue, then, in view of the inflationary consequences of failure to borrow the balance, it is difficult to object when the government uses its powers, notably its powers of taxation, to discriminate in favour of income saved and lent to itself. This justification would disappear the instant the Government went further and used these powers to discriminate in favour of personal income applied to saving generally as against personal income applied to consumption. Hence it would be unsound to extend the tax exemptions[1] of the first £15 of income from certain National Savings (p. 84 f.) to the bottom slice of any other income 'from savings'. Such an exemption could not equitably be limited to the yield on one or two specific kinds of investment, such as trust units, but would in practice have to be spread over the whole of unearned income.

On the same grounds it was economically objectionable, however politically popular, to abolish Schedule A income-tax. As a result of the Finance Act, 1963, there is now tax discrimination in favour of income derived from a specific kind of investment, namely the income in kind from investment in house property. Quite apart from the fact that such property does not necessarily represent in any sense the savings of those who receive the income, the assertion that a person should be taxed on the yield of his savings if, for instance, they are used to create new machinery but not if they are applied to the purchase of a house, needs only to be stated to be seen to be untenable in equity and irrelevant to the promotion of saving. It is true that in strict logic the income in kind arising from the element of saving in other purchases of durable consumer goods, such as private cars, should also be taxed; but in practice, after allowance for maintenance and depreciation, the true income from such savings is comparatively insignificant as well as exceptionally difficult to assess.

[1] From income-tax (for non-surtax payers).

It would be even less justifiable to exempt from tax some or all of the personal income which is applied to 'saving' (however defined), that is, to discriminate for purposes of tax between incomes according not to origin but to outlay. In one sector, indeed, a tax discrimination in favour of income saved (or assumed to be saved) has long existed and has recently been widened:

> relief for life assurance premia and premia on endowment
> assurance policies with a life cover;
> exemption for contributions to approved superannuation funds
> (and for the income of these funds).

It can be argued that these reliefs and exemptions are not discriminations in favour of income saved against other income, but are rather analogous to the tax allowances, such as child allowances, given for expenditures which are a charge upon income. The 'earned income' relief itself has been justified on the ground that since such income is 'precarious', provision must be made out of it for the consequences of its cessation.[1] It was on this line of thought that the Royal Commission, though declaring that an income tax "is more fairly distributed between A and B, having equal incomes and otherwise equal circumstances, if A and B pay the same amount of tax, than if the tax on one of them is lower than the tax on the other because he has reserved part or a larger part of his income from immediate consumption", nevertheless found in favour of the above reliefs and exemptions on the ground that "the man whose income is derived from his personal earnings must in effect regard some provision for his retirement and the care of his dependants as a charge upon those earnings" (l.c. paras. 63, 70). If this reasoning is sufficient to justify something which it is not considered practical politics to reverse, it is also a warning against further extension on the supposed 'principle' of relief for savings.[2]

Besides tax discrimination of various kinds, there is little that the state can do to 'encourage' personal saving—even supposing we make the arbitrary assumption that such saving is less than it 'ought' to be. In the last century, when the Trustee and Post Office Savings Banks were rather a financial burden than otherwise to governments that

---

[1]Royal Commission, Second Report, Cmd. 9105, p. 67.
[2]Investment allowances are not considered here, because they are designed to influence the application and presumably also, like corporation tax, the volume, of *corporate* savings.

could nearly always borrow more than they needed to, the burden was regarded as the price of providing opportunities for small savings. Such opportunities do not today stand in any need of further elaboration by the state. Considering the range of choice, from National Savings of all kinds to unit trusts, and the growing weight of salesmanship, interested or disinterested, behind each alternative, one can scarcely conceive circumstances in which income is spent simply for want of opportunity to save it.

It is true that certain purchases, particularly of securities and real estate, which may represent the application of personal savings, attract a 'turn-over tax' by way of Stamp Duty, and that this impost, which produces about £75 million a year, might conceivably, by reducing the value of the assets of this kind which can be acquired with a given quantity of savings, exert some small effect in altering the distribution of savings, if not in actually reducing the total amount. Though its abolition would hardly have a very significant effect, this is a tax which is not to be justified on the analogy of a turn-over tax on consumption expenditure; for it has the effect of collecting savings as revenue either directly, insofar as the liable transactions represent the application of savings, or indirectly, insofar as they represent the exchange of assets.

There is however one way in which, on past evidence, a government has it in its power to create not only the opportunity but the very strong probability of increased personal saving, and that without either incurring the disadvantages of discrimination between taxpayers or prejudging the 'right' level of saving. It is a method as obvious as it is difficult: to increase the proportion of net to gross personal incomes or, in other words, to reduce the proportion of personal incomes collected in direct taxation. The professions of any government to wish to promote personal saving need not be taken overseriously as long as taxation of incomes is unchanged or increasing.

It is unfortunately impossible to compare the effect on saving of a reduction in taxation of incomes with the effect of a reduction in indirect taxation, or in the level of taxation generally. On the one hand it can be argued *a priori* that indirect taxes levied on items of consumption expenditure increase their cost and thus reduce the margin of personal income which the recipients are willing to save. On the other hand, it might be claimed that any ordinary rise in the cost of consumption goods would not affect the predetermined line between income saved and income laid out on consumption, and might even in some cases deter consumption and increase saving. These hypotheses cannot be tested with the material available; but it seems likely that any effect upon saving of a reduction in indirect taxation must be substantially less than that of an equivalent reduction in direct taxation and increase in disposable net incomes.

It is often alleged that estate duty is a tax specially inimical to the propensity to save. Here again there is no possibility of testing the hypothesis; but the assertion is difficult to accept. It amounts to saying that the recipients of incomes tend to lay more of them out on items of consumption than they would do if the heirs to their estates were going to receive them undiminished or subject to a lesser reduction. To the great mass of contractual saving and to the vast numbers of savers who do not anticipate bequeathing fortunes in excess of the level at which estate duty becomes really appreciable, the question can have no relevance at all. On the other hand, where larger estates than this are accumulated out of income it may reasonably be assumed that, if estate duty loomed large enough to influence behaviour, steps would also be taken, for example by gift *inter vivos*, to transfer the savings to their destination outside the mischief of the duty.

The economic effect of estate duty, as of other taxes on capital, such as a capital gains tax, lies in the destination of the income which is thereby diverted to government use. These are taxes specially likely to be paid not out of income but out of the proceeds of the sale of capital assets. Those proceeds must directly or indirectly come from income which someone else is devoting to the purchase of capital assets, i.e. is saving. The tendency of these taxes is therefore to divert to government use income which would otherwise have gone to increase the assets of the private sector; according to the particular use to which the government applies them, they go either to consumption or to increase the assets of the public sector.

However, the outstanding conclusion for public policy in relation to saving which emerges from this study is a negative one. The importance of rates of interest both for the direction in which savings are applied and for the proportion of income which is saved has repeatedly been argued and illustrated in the foregoing pages. It follows from this that, unless the Government is virtually to plan the whole economy in a manner incompatible with a free society (p. 44), it must refrain from using its powers to influence rates of interest, either with the object of borrowing itself at a lower rate than would otherwise be requisite, or in order to favour certain classes of borrower or promote a predetermined level or pattern of investment.

Index